SYNCOPATED
AN ANTHOLOGY OF NONFICTION PICTO-ESSAYS

EDITED BY
BRENDAN BURFORD

VILLARD
New York

A Villard Books Trade Paperback Original

Syncopated: An Anthology of Nonfiction Picto-Essays is copyright © 2009 by Brendan Burford

Published in the United States by Villard Books,
an imprint of The Random House Publishing Group,
a division of Random House, Inc., New York

ISBN 978-0-345-50529-3

Printed in the United States of America

www.villard.com

2 4 6 8 9 7 5 3 1

Edited and designed by Brendan Burford

SYNCOPATED

AN ANTHOLOGY OF NONFICTION PICTO-ESSAYS

CONTENTS

AN INTRODUCTION

Brendan Burford

―――――――

Welcome to *Syncopated*. As the subtitle indicates, *Syncopated* is an anthology of nonfiction picto-essays. I like this simple description. Although each piece herein represents a different approach, the subtitle aptly describes all of them. These essays range from first-person reportage to historical essay, to profile, to memoir, and even to visual portfolio essay. Each cartoonist represented in *Syncopated* uses the "comics" form or some sort of visual narrative to tell their story, I believe, to great effect.

So, why *Syncopated*? Well, it's a term used to describe a certain quality present in much of the old jazz music I'm personally fond of—syncopation literally means that an accent or stress is placed on the weak beat between the usually dominant beats. When music is syncopated, it can offer a whole new audible perspective on rhythm. I've always thought this was also a good way to describe narrative nonfiction. The contributors in this book are each providing his or her unique perspective on a true story or experience that warranted retelling from a new viewpoint, or with an emphasis on an aspect of the story that may have otherwise gone unnoticed by most people. Each writer is stressing a weak or unaccented beat with their piece.

Another thing I'm fond of is the essay. When I began self-publishing *Syncopated* as a series of stand-alone anthologies, it was around the same time that I was immersing myself in those wonderful old *New Yorker* essayists—E. B. White, Joseph Liebling, John McNulty, and my personal favorite, Joseph Mitchell, among others. I was drawn to the economy of the essay—you can walk away from having read a good essay with a solid understanding of the author's subject without the experience being an exhaustive one. I'm particularly drawn to essays that maintain some level of objectivity without forsaking subjectivity—I believe strongly in authors investing themselves in what they're writing about in order to find greater understanding.

And comics, why *comics*? Why *not* comics—I love comics. (Have you noticed a trend? I love old syncopated music, I love a good essay, I love comics—I'm just selfishly feeding my own interests with this endeavor!) What we've come to call "comics" is a unique and viable medium for storytelling that is inviting on many levels. Comics offer a synesthetic experience through words and pictures that no other medium can.

There are many great examples of comics that offer an accessible point of entry to their language for those who might be uninitiated. Some of them do so without sacrificing their literary value. My hope is that *Syncopated* will join that group through the relatable, well-crafted stories featured within these pages.

HOW and WHY to BALE HAY

When I was thirteen we moved from the city to the country.

The house we moved into was nearly two hundred years old and sat on forty acres of land.

Though a good deal of the land was wet and swampy, there were several fields, an abandoned orchard, and long, overgrown paths that stretched around the property.

And a sturdy old barn made it just right for keeping horses.

My mother was an avid rider and had even ridden her horse to school when she was younger. And she quickly had my sisters riding two older horses she acquired.

My father wasn't thrilled about the amount of food that the horses ate, so Mom decided that next year we'd use the fields to feed the horses.

She started preparing that winter, using a recently-bought International Harvester (1953) to spread the horses' nutrient-rich manure across the fields.

Eww! It's poop!

It seemed a little crazy to my thirteen-year-old self for anyone to spend so much time working on what I felt was a glorified lawn.

Especially after spreading the horse biscuits, the field looked like the polar opposite of the neat Breughel-esque landscapes that I'd imagined the country to be.

Van! Put that down! It's manure!

Eww! You touched poop!

It's warm.

1

Mom decided to lay in Timothy hay.

Phleum pratense

The horses loved it, and it was well-suited to the soil and climate in Southern New England.

Our next-door neighbor, Brett, was also interested in baling his own hay for the horse farm he operated.

Brett had lived on the farm next door his whole life and knew a great deal about growing hay.

"This is a three-point hitch."

"You attach it heah, heah, and heah."

Tilling, the first task to ready the fields, began in early June. This let air and moisture get into the soil, which is why you always see farmers plowing their fields.

In order to spread the very fine Timothy seed, the day has to be just right. If the wind is too high the seed will blow away.

There were many other things to attend to while waiting the six weeks for the hay to grow.

The "Big Field"

My Dad and I spent a lot of time clearing out dead wood that we would burn in our *Franklin stove*, clearing the brush back from the trails, and even trying to *salvage an overgrown* apple orchard.

As a city person who had trimmed the occasional hedge and mowed the lawn now and then, I was unprepared for the fury of **GROWTH** when nature is left to itself.

The apple tree is a good example: when it's left untrimmed it will grow shoots in every direction, choking off its own fruit.

We gave up on the orchard. Pruning and caring for the trees would easily have occupied all of our time.

Coming back from clearing the trails I'd pass through the fields, feeling the grass brush my boots, then my calves, and finally just shy of my hips.

The "Pocket Field"

Now it was time to cut.

You may think that at this point cutting the hay and baling it requires mere brute force and many a tedious circuit around a field, but if the hay is not cut and cured at just the right time, it can easily go to ruin.

The problem is that the hay has to be cut before it dries out and loses its nutritional value.

However, if the hay gets too wet, it runs the risk of composting, which causes the temperature of the interior of the bale to get so hot that it can spontaneously combust--not good for barns.

You hafta jab a metal rod into the bales to check fah heat.

The other difficult factor was lining up the other laborers. I was big enough to help load the bales, but the process requires farmers with special machinery, and many of them would be working their own fields.

So Mom and Brett waited for the window of opportunity, consulting the Farmer's Almanac and listening to weather forecasts and at last the day came for the cutting.

The sickle-bar mower's crossing shears clipped quickly through our fields, but that was the easiest part...

Nails were bitten watching the night skies looking for clues into the next day's weather.

The next day the cut hay would be fluffed up by the Tedder, a whirligig-like device that kicked up, or spun, the hay around, allowing it to dry. This was done at ten in the morning and again at four.

Another worrying evening would pass and the next morning the hay would be windrowed— set up into thin-rowed coils that allow as much air as possible to pass across the hay.

The weather cooperated for that first year's crop and we were all set to start baling at two in the afternoon, the time of day when the hay has the least amount of moisture on it.

The baler picks up the windrowed hay, stuffs it together into a rectangular mass, ties it up lengthwise using two strands of heavy twine and spits it out back onto the field.

The baler we used that first year was old and cranky and Brett had to sit on the rear of the device, tying the second strap of twine around the bale by hand.

Then it was time to pick the bales up.

Side benefit: Mom let me drive the Ford when I was fourteen.

The first year the bales were light and easy to hoist over my head.

Not so the second year when the weather didn't cooperate and the bales were lead weights.

Either way, in order to lift the bale, a hand had to be jabbed under the two strings, and if yours were a pair of dainty 'artist's hands' then they'd scrape up good and quick.

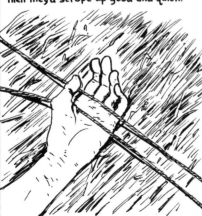

I tried wearing gloves one year, but they were easily caught in the twine.

After grabbing the bale it would have to be hoisted, often above the head, the rough dry stalks scraping against the inside of your forearm.

Setting the bales of hay in the back of the pickup had to have a particular plan since the bales would often stack to twenty feet high, and the Ford would have to travel across bumpy trails and gopher holes.

And by particular plan, I mean that one layer would sit lengthwise and the next would lay cross-wise, repeating for six or seven levels.

We packed the bales tight and never had any fall off on the trips back to the barn.

A highlight of the job was sitting on top of the hay bales and riding over to the barn.

It was a five-minute respite and a view seldom seen from ground-level.

Stacking the bales in the barn was the most difficult part of the operation.

Nary a hint of a breeze wafted past us inside the manure-scented barn.

And clouds of **dust** mingled freely with the sweat on our skin.

I'm not the weakest person in the world, but I'm certainly not the strongest.

I was reminded repeatedly of this as I would hoist a bale to my shoulder, pause, and then fling it as best I could up to the barn attic, while Brett, later my friend Adam, and then a couple of tough kids looking for cash and a workout, would scoop and fling effortlessly.

Only my height, six feet, four inches, gave me any hope of catching up to the other fellas.

Gradually, after several trips, the attic would fill and we'd have to make a passing chain from truck to attic, to the top of the bale mountain.

If we brought in more than one hundred and twenty bales or so, we'd take the surplus over to Brett's cavernous barn and then we were done.

The baling might have taken all of four or five hours, but the heat and dust stretched that short time much longer.

We'd take long swigs from water jugs during the baling, but sitting on the porch, the hay all in, and the sun setting gold on the bulging barn, we'd sip ice-cold tea or cola and nothing has ever tasted so sweet *since.*

Soon though, the shadows predominated and the mosquitos, driven mad with lust by our sweat and deep carbon dioxide-rich exhalations, would force us to part.

And I'd think to myself: "I'll never be Mister Macho, but at least I now have an inkling of the sheer, grinding level of exertion the majority of humankind put forth from sunup to sundown nearly every day."

This felt like a secret to me, a passage into a deeper understanding of life, and a source of great guilt and shame.

I thought of my ancestors, the farmers, the miners, the fishermen, the soldiers, the homemakers, all watching me from the past, and I imagined them clucking: "Try doing that every day 'til you drop!"

From then on every field I pass holds significance to me.

I can see toil and history there, the uprooting of trees, the removal of stones, the constant caretaking, an astounding amount of work.

I see now as far back as Old Anawan himself—perhaps it had been one of my parents' fields where he finally recognized the designs of the Europeans.

It's been twenty years since I last baled hay, that period lasting just five summers.

I went off to college, then back to the city.

Even Brett moved on.

My Mom, now an art teacher, still bales the hay every year with a squad of former students and my Dad still keeps the ever-creeping brush back from the fields.

New (old) tractor

I walked across one of the fields recently, admiring the lack of stones, the hardiness of the soil, the sun-baked smell of manure, and peered into the chaotic beauty of the surrounding forests as I do now whenever I'm in the country.

Can I put MY poop in the field?

Ha!

No.

Baling hay had awakened me to the idea that a field is not an empty void, but rather a swatch of history, of enterprise, and of character.

But WHY can't I?

Horses eat mostly grass so their poop is cleaner than ours.

It only takes a few scratchy, dusty days every summer to hear it.

Clean poop?

The End

8

PENNY SENTIMENTS

by RINA PICCOLO

COLUMBIAN
EXPOSITION
-
CHICAGO
1893

EVERY NOW AND THEN I DISCOVER A FRESH, NEW WAY TO FALL IN LOVE WITH THE PAST.

FOR THE LAST COUPLE OF YEARS I'VE BEEN SEARCHING FOR OLD POSTCARDS. USED ONES.

NEW IN AMERICA
The POSTAL CARD

1 CENT

WATER CLOSETS

MY SEARCH HAS KEPT ME BUSY IN JUNK STORES, ANTIQUE SHOPS, FLEA MARKETS, AND ON E-BAY.

COMMONLY, POSTCARD COL-LECTING CONCERNS ITSELF MAINLY WITH THINGS LIKE PUBLICATION DATES, RARE ISSUES, VALUABLE STAMPS, NOTABLE ART AND PHOTOGRAPHY.

Never breathe a word of this to mother

ain't it cute. I got home Tues. right. Mr. Goodwin may go home next week ERP

MARCH 7
1908

BUT WHAT DREW ME TO THESE "POSTAL CARDS" (AS THEY WERE ONCE CALLED) WERE THE SCRAWLED COMMUNICATIONS ON THEIR BACKS...

POSTAL CARD FOR A MRS. GOODWIN!

AFTER READING A FEW, SOME OVER A CENTURY OLD, I SAW A CERTAIN CHARM IN THESE SEMI-PRIVATE MESSAGES THAT PERHAPS NO OTHER FORM OF EVERYDAY COMMUNICATION CAN CLAIM TO HAVE.

Dear aunt Eliza
Received the chickens and it was very nice. Thanking you very much for it I remain Your Niece
Jennie

MESSAGE WRITTEN ON FRONT OF CARD—A COMMON PRACTICE.
DEC. 6, 1906

POST CARD

Just had another letter from Mabel saying she and Zola would not come until Sunday and wanted me to wait for them to pilot them thru. So can't you go to John's for the day and have him meet us about one and if not there then two sure. Hope you will get this in time to have you make your arrangements all right.
Anna

Dear Harry:
Rec'd your letter this moving and the very thing asked you you never told me I want to know what kind of potatoes you want sent—to plant—and Mrs. Mosher comes to find out for me

Mr. JA Hilone
No 16 Green St.
Scranton

1 CENT

C. 1910

JUL. 28, 1911

LESS FORMAL THAN LETTER-WRITING, AND WITH ITS LIMITED SPACE AND PRIVACY, THE EARLY POSTCARD SAW THE CREATION OF A FORM OF WRITTEN COMMUNICATION THAT WAS ALL ITS OWN.

AS MY COLLECTION GREW SO DID MY KNOWLEDGE OF POST-CARD HISTORY. IT WASN'T LONG BEFORE I UNCOVERED THINGS ABOUT THE EARLY DAYS OF THE POSTCARD THAT REALLY SURPRISED ME.

SAY "WISH YOU WERE HERE"!

DATE UNKNOWN

I WANTED TO SEE MORE OF THESE OLD RELICS NOW THAT I KNEW A LITTLE OF THE PAST FROM WHICH THEY CAME.

THE FIRST POSTCARD AS WE KNOW IT WAS ISSUED IN AUSTRIA IN 1869.

AS A STRICTLY GOVERNMENT-REGULATED POSTAL DEVICE THE POSTCARD MADE ITS DEBUT IN NORTH AMERICA BY THE MID 1870s.

EMPLOYEES ARE FORBIDDEN TO READ POSTAL-CARD MESSAGES

BUT THE REAL HEYDAY OF THE POSTCARD DID NOT ARRIVE UNTIL AN ACT OF CONGRESS WAS PASSED IN 1898 THAT WOULD ALLOW PRIVATE ENTERPRISE COMPLETE FREEDOM IN THE POSTCARD MARKET.

WHAT FOLLOWED WAS A MULTI-MILLION-DOLLAR INDUSTRY FUELED BY A FANATICAL CRAZE.

BUT WHAT OF THE ART OF LETTER-WRITING?

THESE CARDS ARE A **FAD** ...IT WILL SOON PASS.

POSTAL CARD ALBUMS

...THE POSTCARD WAS A HIT.

SOMETIMES WHEN I'M LOOKING AT CARDS FROM THAT TIME ~ BEFORE THE TELEPHONE, BEFORE COMMUNICATION BECAME CHEAP ~ I GET A SENSE OF THAT CRAZE...

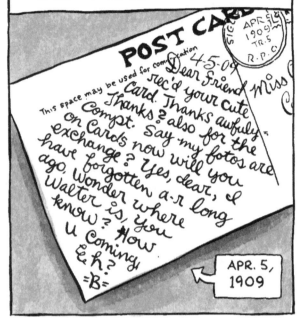

APR. 5, 1909

...AND SOMETIMES I GET A SENSE OF SOMETHING LESS TANGIBLE. ISOLATED AS THEY ARE, THESE FRAGMENTS OF COMMUNICATION HOLD SOME SORT OF MEANING I CAN NEVER QUITE GRASP.

IT'S LIKE READING TOMBSTONES...

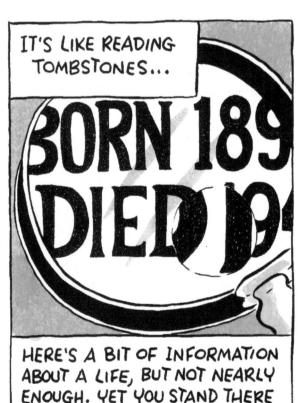

HERE'S A BIT OF INFORMATION ABOUT A LIFE, BUT NOT NEARLY ENOUGH. YET YOU STAND THERE STARING BECAUSE YOU KNOW THERE'S A BODY UNDER IT.

FEB. 15, 1910

©UT OF THE VARIOUS TYPES OF POSTCARDS THAT WERE TRENDY AT THE TURN OF THE CENTURY, THE ONE I FIND MOST EXCITING IS THE **"REAL PHOTO POSTCARD."**

POSTCARD COLLECTORS SALIVATE WHEN THEY SEE AN **"RPP."** THEY ARE ONE OF A KIND—LITERALLY.

IN 1903 THE EASTMAN-KODAK COMPANY PUT ON THE MARKET AN EASY-TO-USE, INEXPENSIVE KIT THAT WOULD MAKE IT POSSIBLE FOR PEOPLE TO TAKE A SNAPSHOT, DEVELOP THE PICTURE ON A CHEMICALLY-TREATED BLANK POSTCARD, AND SEND THE **"REAL PHOTO"** TO FRIENDS AND FAMILY.

Here we are! —xoxo

ALTHOUGH PROFESSIONAL PHOTOGRAPHERS TOOK ADVANTAGE OF THE TREND, A GOOD PORTION OF THESE REAL PHOTO POSTCARDS WERE MADE BY EVERYDAY PEOPLE.

HOW DO YOU WORK THIS THING?

IF ANYTHING THE PHOTOS ARE NOTABLE FOR THEIR HISTORICAL VALUE. THEY DEPICT WORKERS AT WORK, SPORTING EVENTS, PARADES, FIRES, FLOODS, OR PEOPLE JUST POSING FOR THE CAMERA.

REAL PHOTO POSTCARD BERRY PICKERS C. 1910

FOR ME, A REAL PHOTO POSTCARD BRINGS ME CLOSER TO THE PERSON WHOSE HAND-WRITING IS ON THE BACK. I DON'T KNOW WHY LOOKING AT THEM MAKES ME KIND OF SAD...

BOY WITH HANDGUN DATE UNKNOWN

TRAVELLING FAMILY DATE UNKNOWN

...SAD THAT A PERSON'S LIFE CAN BE REDUCED DOWN TO A PIECE OF EPHEMERA.

AS WITH ALL CRAZES THE WHOLE POSTCARD THING GOT A LITTLE RIDICULOUS.

...IMAGINE SENDING YOUR SWEETHEART A POSTCARD MADE OF WOOD, OR METAL.

I'VE YET TO COME ACROSS ANY OF THESE "NOVELTY POSTCARDS," BUT THEY'RE OUT THERE — ALONG WITH CARDS MADE OF BAMBOO, LEATHER, AND IRISH PEAT MOSS, OF ALL THINGS.

YOU COULD EVEN SEND YOUR LOVE IN A SONG ON A GRAMOPHONE POSTCARD.

AND SPEAKING OF SWEETHEARTS, THE POSTCARD WAS AT ONE TIME A WAY TO WOO YOUR LOVER...

MESSAGES WRITTEN UPSIDE-DOWN WERE MEANT TO DISCOURAGE THE POSTMAN'S WANDERING EYE.

QUESTION MARKS APPEAR IN CURIOUS PLACES—LIKE A KNOWING WINK—AND THE SPECIAL POSITIONING OF THE STAMP MEANT SOMETHING IN SECRET CODE THAT THE ADDRESSEE ALONE COULD DECIPHER.

IT'S JUST A **STAMP**, DEAR— WHY ARE YOU BLUSHING?

OTHER SECRETIVE POSTCARDS WERE NOT AS INNOCENT. LIKE THE CASES I READ ABOUT IN WHICH EMBOSSED POSTCARDS HAD BEEN USED FOR THE SMUGGLING OF COCAINE AND MORPHINE.

ILY ★ GAZE

POSTAL CARDS PROHIBITED IN TURKEY

INSURANCE POSTAL CARDS AVAILABLE TO TRAVELE

"NAUGHTY" POSTAL CARDS NOT ALLOWED THROUGH MAIL

CONTEST WINNER 10,000 WORDS ON SING CARD!

ON E-BAY YOU CAN BID ON A SINGLE POSTCARD, OR ON WHAT'S CALLED AN "EPHEMERA LOT" — A BUNCH OF ODDS AND ENDS MIXED IN WITH POSTCARDS. I LIKE THESE THE BEST BECAUSE THEY'RE LIKE THE SURPRISE BAGS I USED TO GAMBLE ON WITH MY TEN CENTS AS A KID.

ESTATE SALE
OCT 9, 2007

FOR AS LITTLE AS THIRTY BUCKS I CAN OWN ONE OF THESE LOTS...

NOT KNOWING WHAT I MIGHT FIND I GO THROUGH THE CARDS, READING THEIR MESSAGES AS THOUGH THE PEOPLE WHO WROTE THEM STOPPED BEING DEAD FOR AN EVENING SO THEY COULD TALK TO ME.

INSCRIBED "ANNIE MURPHY" DATE UNKNOWN

SOMETIMES WHAT THEY SAY CAN BE CREEPY...

THIS SPACE FOR WRITING MESSAGES

Miss F.A. Weath
336 Broad
Waverly

They found that girl that got drowned near this bridge this am. Wed.

C. 1910

...I NEVER IMAGINED A GIRL'S TRAGIC DEATH COULD BE A GREETING ON THE BACK OF A SOUVENIR POSTCARD.

OTHER TIMES I HAVE A LAUGH. IN ONE CARD THE NEUROTIC RAMBLINGS OF A WOMAN ARE HAULED OUT OF THE PAST. AS IF NOT EVEN DEATH COULD SHUT HER UP.

Monday # 6 + 'last' on train Fran
If you get this in time won't Tib Please sign on the meal slip outsi office de name under presen
for din taken dow
at 8pm you don
get thi n time
present lunch "u
for Thurs of the X-m
eve party is to include dinner "out for dinner" — I know this is very comp licated and if you haven't time to sign for Wednesday dinner I'll eat soup and eggs — only leav 1905 a note

BARELY LEGIBLE 129-WORD MESSAGE ABOUT DINNER ARRANGEMENTS

MANY OF THE MESSAGES, ESPECIALLY THOSE FROM THE EARLY 1900s, HAVE A TONE SIMILAR TO TODAY'S E-MAILS. I'M ABLE TO DISCERN FROM THE POSTMARKS THAT MAIL SERVICE WAS AMAZINGLY EFFICIENT.

"WILL YOU COME TO TEA AT 4?"

WITH UP TO FIVE LOCAL DELIVERIES PER DAY, IT WAS POSSIBLE TO SEND A POSTCARD IN THE MORNING AND HAVE IT RECEIVED BY NOON.

...AND I HAVE TO WONDER WHEN I SEE A CARD POSTMARKED "DEC. 25," OR "6 AM"

...DID THE POSTCARD HAVE SPECIAL PRIVILEGES?

NOV. 12, 1909

JUNE 24, 1913

17

THERE IS NO DOUBT THAT BEFORE WIDESPREAD USE OF THE TELEPHONE THE POSTCARD WAS THE CHEAPEST METHOD FOR LOCAL AND LONG-DISTANCE COMMUNICATION.

IT'S TOUCHING TO READ ABOUT THE DAY-TO-DAY LIVES OF FAMILIES SEPARATED BY WAR, EMPLOYMENT, AND OTHER LIFE-CHANGING EVENTS THAT PUT MILES BETWEEN PEOPLE.

I LIKE TO IMAGINE THAT THESE POSTCARDS OF MINE ARE DROPS FROM AN UNTAPPED PAST—LARGER THAN THE SUM OF ITS PARTS.

IF WE COULD LINE UP CHRONO-LOGICALLY EVERY POSTCARD EVER SENT, WOULD WE SEE ANOTHER HISTORY EMERGE?

BORIS ROSE : PRISONER OF JAZZ

BY BRENDAN B. & JIM CAMPBELL

Boris Rose's introduction to jazz music began as a young boy in the early 1930's when he heard the big bands of that period for the first time.

He would eagerly tune into the radio broadcasts of live performances by Duke Ellington's band and Benny Goodman's, and Cab Calloway's among others.

His love of early Jazz grew to include dance bands of the 1920's and early 1930's.

Around 1940, Boris began dubbing 78RPM records on to 10-inch red vinyl disks with hand-written white labels.

He would sell these dubs of Jelly Roll Morton, King Oliver, Louis Armstrong, and other great early jazz musicians to anyone interested in buying them.

This would be the beginning of a life-long obsession with making recordings for the sake of preservation and—illegally or not—for profit.

After his release from the military in 1946, Boris continued dubbing 78's, but noticed a growing apathy toward the traditional jazz he himself was so fond of.

The late 1940's saw the rise of the Be Bop era of Jazz.

The legendary Coleman Hawkins paved an early path for Charlie Parker, Dizzy Gillespie, and Bud Powell.

Performances from New York City's newest Be Bop jazz clubs were broadcast live over the radio regularly by this time.

Although Boris didn't particularly care for Be Bop, he was astute enough to recognize that it was a relevant and historically important movement.

He was committed to documenting the ascent of this new idiom in jazz music.

By this time, Boris had acquired recording equipment that could capture radio broadcasts to large 16-inch disks.

The Be Bop broadcasts came over the airwaves from clubs like the Royal Roost, and Birdland, and Bop City.

Many of these broadcasts would take place from three to four o'clock in the morning, and Boris would set his alarm clock for 2:45am in order to prepare his recording equipment.

Boris couldn't always get the cleanest transmission from his apartment on East 10th Street in New York's East Village. So he would often set up at friends' places closer to Midtown.

He methodically logged each performance date, its venue and its personnel into a series of bound ledgers.

The obsession had taken a firm hold over him.

Over the years Boris captured thousands of hours of recordings that likely did not exist anywhere else -- his was easily the largest private collection of its kind anywhere in the world.

Eventually Boris began recording every sort of broadcast imaginable -- he even recorded the soundtracks of entire movies as they were broadcast over television.

When long playing records came into existence, Boris began dubbing some of his recordings for commercial sale.

The covers and liner notes for these records, if they existed at all, were purposefully vague, as if Boris knew what he was doing wasn't exactly legal.

He made up all sorts of names and images for labels that would be difficult to trace back to him. He even went so far as using Swedish words for the songs, which were meant to appear as Swedish translations, but were in fact random words from a Swedish tourist phrase book.

RADIEX
LESTER YOUNG

Okidoke RECORDS
DUKE ELLINGTON

Bamboo RECORDS
BILLIE HOLIDAY

AXTOR

The basement and first floor of the East 10th Street building, which he now owned, was filled with likely fifty or sixty thousand LP's in addition to all of his 16-inch acetates and red vinyl disks.

Boris eventually began recording with magnetic tape, but not for several years after it became a viable recording medium.

He claimed the quality was inferior -- which was true. By the late 1970's, Boris began to slow down his pace of recording.

Live broadcasting of worthwhile jazz had become a thing of the past and Boris didn't feel compelled to continue documenting what he heard.

He continued to issue more and more of his LP transfers, but to this day, somewhere around 95% of all his material has not been issued.

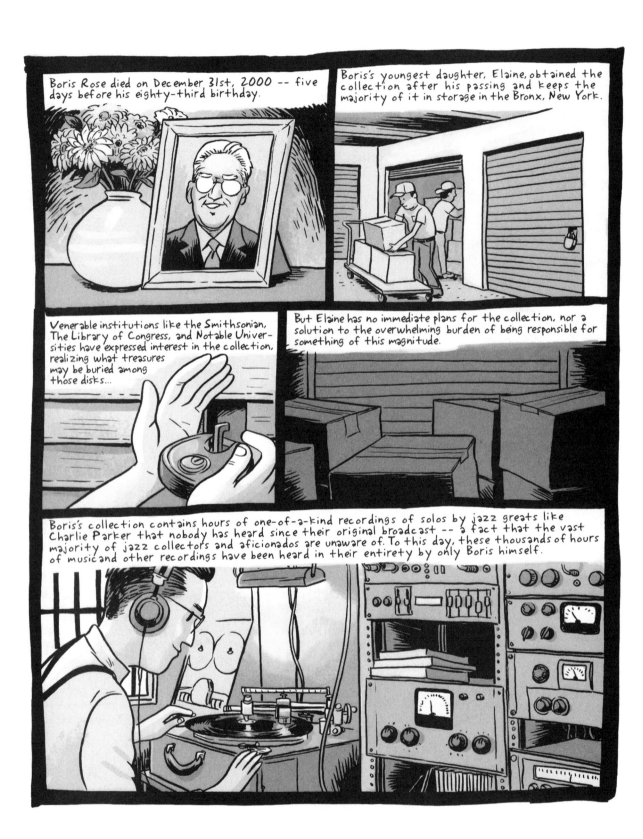

Boris Rose died on December 31st, 2000 -- five days before his eighty-third birthday.

Boris's youngest daughter, Elaine, obtained the collection after his passing and keeps the majority of it in storage in the Bronx, New York.

Venerable institutions like the Smithsonian, The Library of Congress, and Notable Universities have expressed interest in the collection, realizing what treasures may be buried among those disks...

But Elaine has no immediate plans for the collection, nor a solution to the overwhelming burden of being responsible for something of this magnitude.

Boris's collection contains hours of one-of-a-kind recordings of solos by jazz greats like Charlie Parker that nobody has heard since their original broadcast -- a fact that the vast majority of jazz collectors and aficionados are unaware of. To this day, these thousands of hours of music and other recordings have been heard in their entirety by only Boris himself.

PORTFOLIO
BY TRICIA VAN DEN BERGH

"Omnia mutantur, nihil interit." —Ovid

I began this series of Washington Square Park illustrations in June of 2006 as a standard sketchbook exercise in life drawing. They are small, quick studies of the park itself, excluding people and crowds. To keep a bit of consistency, they were all drawn at dusk, enabling me to muddle around with some unique lighting.

Its sordid history aside, I chose Washington Square Park simply because it's a personal favorite haunt of mine. It offers a sense of well-being that only a plot of manicured wilderness can possibly give. Over time, I became ever-more intimate with its black locust, maple, and elm. However, autumn of 2007 had brought changed leaves of a different sort to my little refuge. Nearly half the park had been closed off due to renovation. On behalf of the New York City Parks Department, Washington Square Park would be restored to its former 1870s layout. Needless to say, this kicked up a row with many of the park's frequent visitors, myself included. Politics and nostalgic memories were points of contention for me, but more myopically, I objected to the fact that the chance to sketch certain areas of the park was forever lost to me.

It's absurd to me now that I thought this park was impervious to change, and that my initial feelings were of ill will toward its change. Every place is in a state of flux and attempts to document this phenomenon are fleeting. Although the emphasis in these drawings is on environment, I believe, for the time being, this place remains Washington Square Park not because of its fashionable landscaping of the day but because of its constant cast of characters—the performers, musicians, chess players, locals, students, even those pesky tourists, and everyone else in between.

As I was growing up, basically raised by my mom, a lot of men passed through my life...

FATHER FIGURES

by JOSH '08

AGE 2: DAD TAKES OFF.

I JUST DON'T THINK I'M CUT OUT TO BE A FATHER.

AGE 3: UNCLEAR ON THE CONCEPT.

DA-DA?

Celery.

4-5: REUBEN. A DOCTOR WHO LIKED MY MOM AND MY DRAWINGS.

6: DAD, BACK FOR A VISIT. SCARED THE CAT.

HELLO, I'M YOUR FATHER.

MRRAOWWW

7: DANIEL. JUMPED OUR CAR BATTERY. ASKED FOR MY MOM'S NUMBER, WHICH I SHOUTED OUT. MOM NOT THRILLED--BUT HE TOOK US OUT TO A NICE MEAL.

7-11: ALLAN. ARGUED MARX WITH MY MOM OVER DINNER.

8: DAD, WITH WIFE #2, TOOK ME IN FOR A YEAR. BOUGHT ME COMICS, REMOVED A SPLINTER, TOOK ME TO SEE "BLAZING SADDLES."

9-11: AUSTIN & PAUL, HOUSE-MATES. TOOK ME TO THE BEACH, PLAYED PRANKS--TREATED ME LIKE THEIR LITTLE BROTHER.

"I SEE," SAID THE BLIND MAN.

34

9-11: PHIL, OUR OTHER HOUSE-MATE. TAPPED HIS CEREAL DOWN BELOW THE MILK. USED KETCHUP AND MAYO TO MAKE SMILEY-FACES ON HIS BURGER PATTIES.

9-13: DAD, FOR A MONTH EACH SUMMER. FED ME STEAK AND CHICKEN, TAUGHT ME TO PLAY BASEBALL.

THAT'S IT-- KEEP YOUR EYE ON THE BALL!

11-13: BOB. TOOK ME TO CANDLESTICK PARK. CHAMPIONED LITTLE LEAGUE, BARBER HAIRCUTS, ADIDAS SNEAKERS.

13: MICHAEL. GRAD STUDENT WHO HUNG AROUND A WHILE...

14-17: DAD, WITH WIFE #3 AND NEW BABY. TOOK ME IN FOR HIGH SCHOOL.

14-20: HAWKEYE. CRACKED WISE, YET ABLE TO CRY. LOVED-- AND RESPECTED--WOMEN.

MY KIDNEYS WERE EXPECTING ORANGE JUICE. **SILLY** KIDNEYS.

14-21: JOHN. CAME WITH A DOG AND A COUNTRY HOUSE. TAUGHT ME TO PLAY SQUASH.

THERE YOU GO-- KEEP YOUR EYE ON THE BALL!

AGE 40: JOSH. $(DAD^5 \div WIVES^2)$ $+ (MOM \div BOYFRIENDS^7) \times (DOG + HOUSEMATES^3) \div (BASEBALL + COMICS) \times (CELERY + STEAK) \times ("BLAZING SADDLES" + "M*A*S*H")$

EQUALS ...?

ME!

DA-DA!

Phoebe, 10 months

WEST SIDE IMPROVEMENTS
BY
ALEX HOLDEN

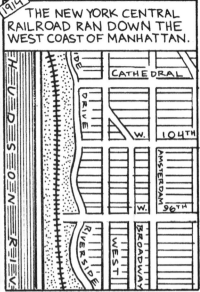

1914 THE NEW YORK CENTRAL RAILROAD RAN DOWN THE WEST COAST OF MANHATTAN.

RUNNING IN A DEEP TRENCH, THE RAILROAD EFFECTIVELY CUT OFF RIVERSIDE PARK FROM THE WATERFRONT.

THE PARTS OF THE PARK THAT WERE NOT SINKING BACK INTO THE HUDSON WERE PILED WITH COAL FOR THE TRAINS AND GARBAGE BOUND FOR THE DUMP.

SHANTY TOWNS TOO DANGEROUS EVEN FOR THE POLICE LINED THE TRACKS.

SMOKE FILLED THE SKY ALONG WITH THE STENCH OF LIVE-STOCK ON THE WAY TO THE SLAUGHTER-HOUSE.

A YOUNG ROBERT MOSES DREAMT OF RECLAIMING THE PARK FOR THE PEOPLE OF NEW YORK.

IT WAS NOT MOSES' IDEA TO COVER THE TRACKS. IT HAD BEEN PROPOSED BEFORE BUT NO ONE COULD GET THE PROJECT COMPLETED.

PROPOSED DRIVE AND PARKWAY

TRACKS

1891

PROPOSED DEVELOPMENT TRACKS 86-93 STREETS

1910

TWENTY YEARS LATER, MOSES HAD CAREFULLY ACQUIRED AN UNSTOPPABLE AMOUNT OF POWER.

WITHOUT A DOUBT

ON YOUR DESK

ON ITS WAY

YES SIR

ABSOLUTELY

RIGHT AWAY

YES SIR

THROUGH SOME CREATIVE FINANCING, HE MANAGED TO JUMPSTART THE LONG-STALLED "WEST SIDE IMPROVEMENT."

PUBLIC ART FUND

CIVIL WORKS ADMIN

PUBLIC WORKS ADMIN

FEDERAL RIVERS AND HARBORS ACT

RAIL ROAD

USING FILL FROM THE 8TH AVE SUBWAY EXCAVATION, 500 TRUCKLOADS A DAY, 75 ACRES WERE ADDED TO RIVERSIDE PARK.

THE TRACKS WERE COVERED FROM 72ND ST TO 125TH ST: THE EDGE OF HARLEM.

CLANG
CLANG
CLANG
CLANG
CLANG
CLANG
CLANG

ON OCTOBER 12, 1937, THE WEST SIDE IMPROVEMENT WAS COMPLETED TO MUCH FANFARE.

"NEW MASTER-PIECE OUT OF ROBERT MOSES' ATELIER"

"THE MOST BEAUTIFUL DRIVE IN THE WORLD"

"A FOUNTAIN OF HEALTH AND PLEASURE..."

TODAY, MANY PEOPLE DON'T EVEN KNOW ABOUT THE TRACKS UNDER THE PARK.

THE ONLY SIGNS FROM ABOVE ARE THE GRATED VENTS.

ALONG A CERTAIN STRETCH OF THE PARK, EACH GRATE REVEALS A SILVER AND BLACK PAINTING ON THE WALL OF THE TUNNEL.

ONE NONDESCRIPT AREA HOUSES SEVERAL GRATES IN A ROW.

THIS SERIES OF GRATES ILLUMINATES AN ENORMOUS NINE PANEL MURAL IN THE TUNNEL.

THE MURAL IS THE CULMINATION OF YEARS OF WORK IN THE TUNNEL BY CHRIS PAPE.

SELF PORTRAIT CIRCA 1982

IN 1974, CHRIS, HIS BROTHER, VINCE, AND THEIR FRIENDS SPENT THEIR TIME WRITING THEIR NAMES ON TRAINS AND WALLS. THEY CALLED THEMSELVES "THE ACID WRITERS."

MANNY "CLOUD 9"

CHRIS "GEN 2"

VINCE "LSD 2001"

IN THE MID 70'S, NEW YORK WAS IN SHAMBLES. CHRIS COULD OFTEN BE FOUND PLAYING IN AN ABANDONED CONSTRUCTION SITE,

READY?

JUMP!

HANGING OUT IN THE SUBWAY STATION, WATCHING THE TRAINS GO BY,

CLIMBING TREES IN CENTRAL PARK,

FARTHER!!

OR EXPLORING THE FREIGHT TUNNEL UNDER RIVERSIDE PARK.

THE ACID WRITERS PREFERRED TO ENTER THE TUNNEL THROUGH A HOLE IN THE 88TH STREET BATHROOM.

A WRITER NAMED STEVE 161 HAD STOLEN SOME DYNAMITE FROM A CONSTRUCTION SITE AND BLOWN A HOLE IN THE FLOOR.

BOOM

SLIDING DOWN THE EMBANK-
MENT WAS MORE FUN THAN
TAKING THE STAIRCASES THAT
THEY LATER FOUND AND
IGNORED.

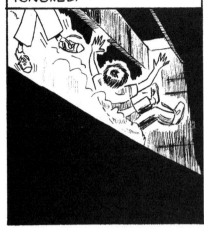

IF THEY HAD PAINT, THEY
WOULD PRACTICE THEIR
SIGNATURES. OTHERWISE
THEY WOULD ADMIRE OTHER
WRITERS' WORK, OR MAYBE
ATTEMPT TO DO SOME OF
THEIR OWN WORK ON A
DORMANT FREIGHT CAR.

BY 1976, GEN TWO FADED
FROM THE GRAFFITI
WORLD AS CHRIS FINISHED
HIGH SCHOOL.

IN 1979, CHRIS RE-EMERGED
WITH A NEW NAME: FREEDOM.

WHILE PAINTING HIS NAME
ON A SUBWAY CAR, HE
REALIZED THAT HE COULD
SHADE BY MISTING BLACK
PAINT OVER SILVER PAINT.

HMMM..

TSSSSS
TSS
TSS

SEVERAL PORTRAIT
EXPERIMENTS FOLLOWED.

LOOKS LIKE
LENNY BRUCE.

JAMES
DEAN

ONE DAY, CHRIS NOTICED
SOME JOGGERS LOOKING
INTO THE VENTS OF THE
FREIGHT TUNNEL.

HE REALIZED THAT THE
WALL SEEN FROM THE VENT
COULD ALSO BE SEEN
THROUGH OPENINGS ON
THE SIDE OF THE TUNNEL.

HMM...
I GOTTA PAINT
SOMETHING
DOWN THERE

SOME-
THING
BIG.

HIS RENDITION MADE THE
VILLAGE VOICE, BUT HE
WOULD NOT PAINT THE
TUNNEL AGAIN FOR A YEAR.

BY 1981, FREEDOM HAD BEGUN SHOWING IN ART GALLERIES ALONG WITH SOME OTHER GRAFFITI WRITERS.

WHEN HIS FRIENDS RECEIVED A COMMISSION WITHOUT HIM, FREEDOM WROTE A SEVEN PAGE ILLUSTRATED STORY CALLED "'TWAS THE NIGHT BEFORE DOOMSDAY" AND PAINTED IT ON A LONG STRETCH OF TUNNEL WALL WITH CONSISTENT LIGHTING.

THIS WAS THE FIRST AMBITIOUS WORK THAT HE WOULD PAINT ON THIS PARTICULAR STRETCH OF WALL. TODAY, THE NINE PANEL "BUY AMERICAN" MURAL CAN BE FOUND HERE.

FOR THE NEXT SEVERAL YEARS, FREEDOM REGULARLY VISITED THE TUNNEL. PORTRAITS, RE-CREATIONS OF FAMOUS ARTWORKS, TRIBUTES AND MEMORIALS ALL LINED THE WALLS IN HIS SIGNATURE SILVER AND BLACK PAINT.

THE FREIGHT COMPANY HAD ABANDONED THE TUNNEL, LEAVING FREEDOM TO WORK IN RELATIVE SOLITUDE.

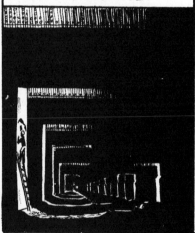

HIS ABOVEGROUND GALLERY CAREER SLOWED DOWN.

WELL.. I DON'T KNOW..

IT'S TOO ABSTRACT..

IT NEEDS TO BE MORE

YOU KNOW

GRAFFITI

SOME COLORFUL LETTERS

HE CONTINUED TO ENJOY HIS PRIVATE UNDERGROUND GALLERY UNTIL 1986.

OH MAN.. IS THAT A BED?

SOON AFTER

HEY MAN..

41

CHRIS HAD BEEN IN COLLEGE OFF AND ON SINCE 1980. IN 1986, HE SWITCHED HIS MAJOR FROM ILLUSTRATION TO VISUAL JOURNALISM.

HE DREW ALL OVER THE CITY.

OF COURSE, HE ENDED UP BACK IN THE TUNNEL. HE OFTEN DREW BY BERNARD'S FIRE, A SOCIAL HUB IN THE TUNNEL.

HE EVENTUALLY COMPLETED WELL OVER 600 DRAWINGS.

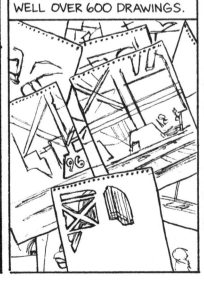

AS HE SPENT MORE TIME WITH THE TUNNEL RESIDENTS, HE BEGAN TO RETHINK HIS ROLE DOWN THERE.

HIS PRIVATE GALLERY HAD BECOME A HOME TO SEVERAL HUNDRED PEOPLE.

DURING THIS TIME, ANOTHER NAME HAD STARTED TO APPEAR IN THE TUNNEL.

DAVID AND ROGER SMITH WERE TWO BROTHERS, NOTORIOUS FOR WRITING SANE (AND) SMITH THROUGHOUT NEW YORK CITY.

Vandalism Draws Ire

By Kevin Flynn

WHILE ROGER ATTENDED FORDHAM UNIVERSITY, DAVID WOULD OFTEN CUT CLASS TO PAINT, OR SIMPLY TO SOCIALIZE IN THE TUNNEL.

HAS FREEDOM BEEN BY LATELY?

HEY, PULL UP A CHAIR.

YEAH. HE WAS JUST HERE DRAWING. MAYBE NEXT TIME

SANE WAS QUITE RESPECTFUL OF FREEDOM'S WORK. HE RESTRICTED HIS WORK TO THE ALCOVES, LEAVING FREEDOM'S WALLS UNINTERRUPTED.

CHRIS AVOIDED THE BROTHERS AT FIRST, BUT MEETING THEM WAS INEVITABLE. THEY BEGAN TO PAINT TOGETHER OCCASIONALLY.

I COULD DO A PORTRAIT IN THE MIDDLE MAYBE?

COULD BE GOOD..

IN 1990, KEITH HARING DIED. WITH A FEW MUTUAL FRIENDS, FREEDOM HELPED PAINT A MEMORIAL FOR HARING, FEEDING HIS GROWING INTEREST IN COLLABORATION.

I THINK THAT LOOKS BETTER.

ME TOO.

IN THE TUNNEL, LESS RESPECTFUL WRITERS BEGAN TO MAKE THEIR PRESENCE KNOWN.

WE NEED TO GET THIS KID

I DON'T KNOW, ROGER...

ON OCTOBER 25, 1990, THE BODY OF DAVID SMITH WAS FOUND FLOATING IN THE NARROWS OFF THE BAY RIDGE SECTION OF BROOKLYN.

ROGER RODE THE 1 TRAIN FROM THE BEGINNING TO THE END OF THE LINE, SCATTERING HIS BROTHER'S ASHES.

HE SAVED SOME OF THE ASHES FOR CHRIS TO SCATTER BENEATH A PAINTING IN THE TUNNEL.

CHRIS BROUGHT THE ASHES HOME, WAITING FOR THE RIGHT MOMENT.

MEANWHILE, AMTRAK HAD TAKEN OVER THE TUNNEL. SOON ENOUGH, PASSENGER TRAINS BARRELLED THROUGH AT DANGEROUS SPEEDS.

ROAR!

IN 1992, SMITH AND FREEDOM DECIDED TO COLLABORATE ON A PAINTING FOR BERNARD. FREEDOM SUGGESTED PICASSO'S "GUERNICA".

HE LIKED THE IDEA OF PEOPLE LIVING IN FRONT OF THE PAINTING, MAKING THEM A LIVING PART OF THE PIECE.

SMITH PROPOSED GOYA'S "THE THIRD OF MAY." INTRIGUED BY HOW BERNARD'S FIRE ECHOED THE LIGHTING OF THE PAINTING, FREEDOM AGREED.

BERNARD HELPED THE TWO ARTISTS PRIME THE WALL.

THE PAINTING WAS COMPLETED OVER SEVERAL FREEZING DAYS.

ONE DAY WHEN THEY WERE LEAVING, SMITH PAINTED "FREEDOM" ABOVE THE ENTRY WAY, DUBBING IT "THE FREEDOM TUNNEL."

THE NAME STUCK. TO THIS DAY, PEOPLE STILL REFER TO "THE FREEDOM TUNNEL."

IN 1993, A BOOK CALLED <u>THE MOLE PEOPLE</u> WAS PUBLISHED. A LARGE PORTION OF THE BOOK FOCUSED ON THE RESIDENTS OF THE TUNNEL.

THE BOOK SPARKED A MEDIA FRENZY.

TELEVISION CREWS BECAME A COMMON SIGHT IN THE TUNNEL.

DO YOU LIKE BEING CALLED A MOLE PERSON?

SOON, CHRIS HAD A FULL-TIME JOB AS A GUIDE TO THE TUNNEL AND A LIAISON BETWEEN THE MEDIA AND THE "MOLE PEOPLE".

THIS IS WHERE BERNARD LIVES.

IS HE HERE?

PERHAPS DUE TO THE MEDIA CIRCUS, AMTRAK ANNOUNCED THAT IT WAS EVICTING EVERYONE FROM THE TUNNEL IN ONE YEAR'S TIME.

WITH THIS DEADLINE LOOMING, CHRIS WANTED TO DO ONE FINAL PAINTING THAT SUMMED EVERYTHING UP.

THE STARTING POINT WAS A PHOTO BY MARGARET BOURKE-WHITE OF FLOOD VICTIMS LINED UP FOR AID UNDER A BILLBOARD.

THE PHOTOGRAPH WAS TAKEN IN 1937.

SIXTY YEARS LATER, NOTHING HAD CHANGED, AS CHRIS PASSED BY SOUP KITCHENS EVERY DAY.

HE DECIDED TO PAINT THE BILLBOARD WITHOUT THE BREADLINE. HE DIDN'T NEED IT. THE TUNNEL RESIDENTS WOULD FILL THAT ROLE.

THE MURAL HAS NINE PANELS. ON THE LEFT-HAND SIDE IS A SANE PIECE ON A SUBWAY CAR.

THIS PORTION OF THE MURAL WAS PAINTED BY ROGER SMITH.

A PORTRAIT OF BERNARD, THE SELF-PROCLAIMED "LORD OF THE TUNNEL" AND CHRIS' FRIEND.

THE COCA COLA AD HAS SEVERAL MEANINGS. REFERENCING AMERICAN CONSUMERISM, THE INTRODUCTION OF "NEW COKE" AT THE HEIGHT OF THE CRACK EPIDEMIC, AND ANOTHER GRAFFITI WRITER WHO EXPLORED THE TUNNEL IN THE 1970'S : COCA 82.

THE HAPPY FAMILY FROM THE BOURKE-WHITE PHOTOGRAPH.

A REFERENCE TO THE MOLE PEOPLE PHENOMENON.

DROP THE GUN MOLE!

AK!

"THERE'S NO WAY LIKE THE AMERICAN WAY," ALSO FROM THE PHOTOGRAPH.

NEVER COMPLETED, THE SEVENTH PANEL CONTAINS SEVERAL MISSILES, WHICH, IF LAUNCHED, WOULD LAND ON THE FAMILY IN PANEL FOUR.

A PORTRAIT OF BOB, ANOTHER TUNNEL RESIDENT THAT CHRIS HAD COME TO KNOW OVER THE YEARS.

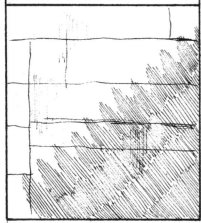

THESE RED AND WHITE STRIPES BALANCE THE STRIPES IN THE SANE PIECE AND ECHO THE RED COKE PANEL, AS WELL AS IMPLYING THE AMERICAN FLAG.

WHEN THE PAINTING WAS FINISHED, CHRIS SCATTERED SANE'S ASHES ALONG THE LENGTH OF THE MURAL.

THE EVICTION WAS DELAYED BUT INEVITABLE.

THE GOVERNMENT EARMARKED EIGHT MILLION DOLLARS TO HOUSE THE EVICTED.

WORKING WITH PHOTOGRAPHER MARGARET MORTON AND THE COALITION FOR THE HOMELESS, CHRIS TRIED TO HELP RE-LOCATE THE TUNNEL DWELLERS.

MANY WERE RETICENT TO LEAVE THE TUNNEL, BUT SOME EVENTUALLY ACCEPTED THE OFFER.

AROUND THIS TIME, FREEDOM ADDED A BLOCK OF TEXT TO THE FLAG SECTION OF THE FINAL SPRAWLING MURAL.

IN DECEMBER 1995 THE FORGOTTEN MEN OF THE TUNNEL RECIEVED "CITY HOUSING" THEY'VE JUST BEGUN TO MOVE —"F"

EVENTUALLY, AMTRAK KEPT ITS WORD, WELDING EVERY ENTRANCE CLOSED.

GOD DAMN IT

RATTLE RATTLE RATTLE

ONCE THE TUNNEL WAS SEALED OFF, CHRIS HAD LITTLE INTEREST IN PAINTING DOWN THERE.

AS OF THIS WRITING, MANY OF HIS WORKS ARE STILL VISIBLE.

ROBERT MOSES HAD COVERED THE RAILROAD TRACKS TO EXPAND AND IMPROVE RIVERSIDE PARK.

HE ALSO LAID THE GROUND-WORK FOR A HISTORIC UNDER-GROUND ART GALLERY.

SELECTED SOURCES
- INTERVIEW WITH CHRIS PAPE: MARCH 25, 2008 & APRIL 24, 2008
- THE POWER BROKER BY R. CARO
- THE TUNNEL BY M. MORTON
- ROBERT MOSES AND THE MODERN CITY EDITED BY H. BALLON AND K.T. JACKSON
- THE MOLE PEOPLE BY J. TOTH
- NEW YORK CENTRAL RAILROAD BY B. SOLOMON WITH M. SCHAFER
- NEW YORK TIMES 1/17/17 P.5
- NEW YORK TIMES 2/28/35 P.11
- NEW YORK TIMES 2/29/36 P.17
- NEW YORK PUBLIC LIBRARY IMAGE COLLECTION
- SPRAYCAN ART BY H. CHALFANT AND J. PRIGOFF
- HIP HOP FILES BY M. COOPER
- AEROSOL KINGDOM BY I.L. MILLER
- SUBWAY GRAFFITI BY J. STEWART

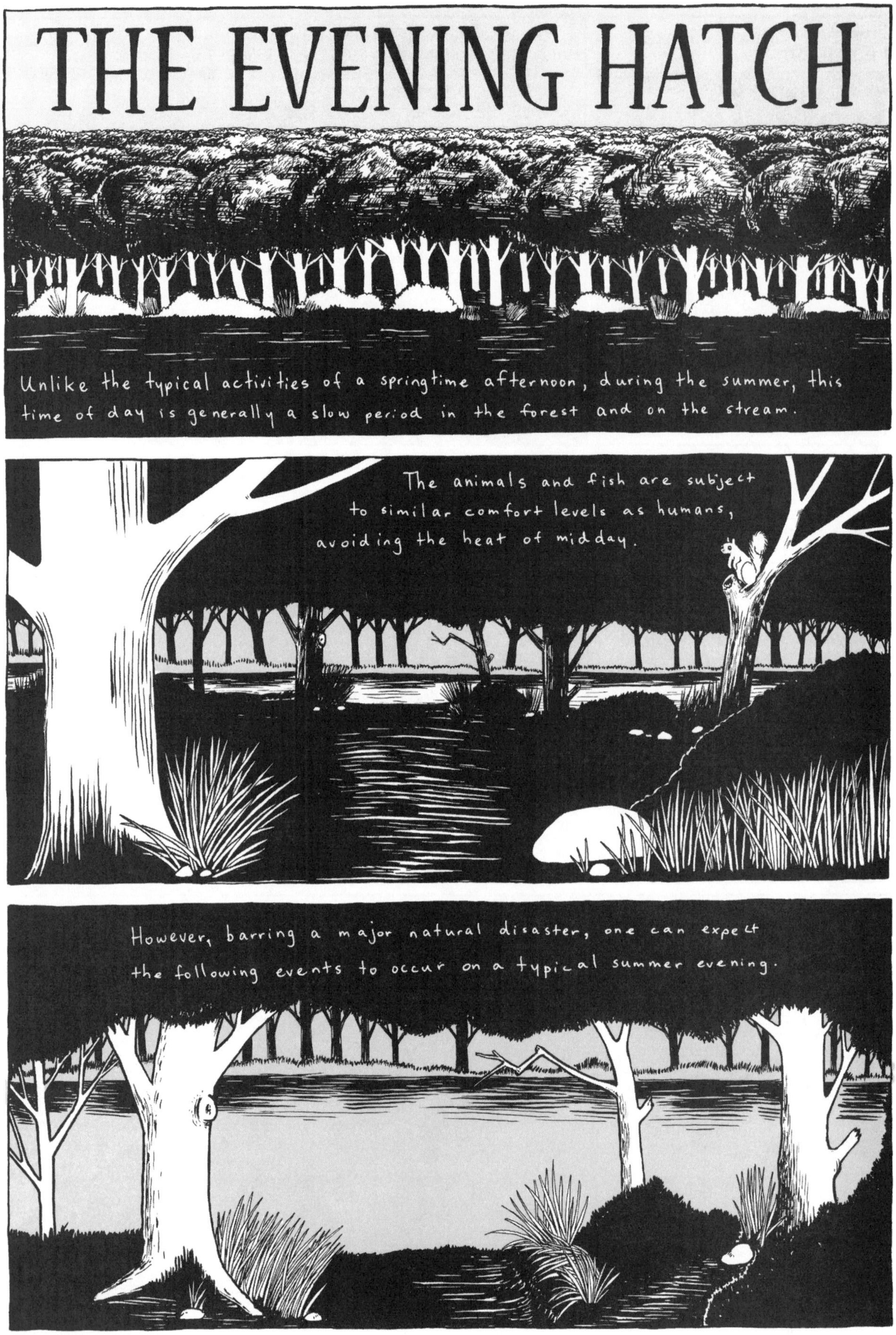
THE EVENING HATCH
Unlike the typical activities of a springtime afternoon, during the summer, this time of day is generally a slow period in the forest and on the stream.
The animals and fish are subject to similar comfort levels as humans, avoiding the heat of midday.
However, barring a major natural disaster, one can expect the following events to occur on a typical summer evening.

As the afternoon progresses, the sun begins to fall behind the trees and sunlight leaves the water.

The creatures of the forest and the stream return as the day's high temperatures fall.

A flyfisherman arrives and doesn't immediately begin to fish, but watches as the events unfold.

The trout in the stream hold their position as the fly fisherman attempts to ascertain what they might be feeding on that night.

Blue Wing Olive mayflies drift down the river and waxwing birds fly about, gathering the emerging flies as they take flight.

Soon, the tan and black Caddis flies return from the streamside brush and begin their erratic mating flight along the stream's surface.

The trout begin to find their rhythm as the Blue Wing Olives accelerate their arrival or the "hatch."

Sexually active flies buzz over the stream, and while the females lay their eggs, the "spent" males drop to the water's surface.

The trout gluttonously engorge themselves on their evening meal.

The stream is alive with swarms of flies, jumping fish and hungry bats.

The cacophony of activity crescendos at dusk and generally lasts fifteen to thirty minutes.

Then all of a sudden, as if someone turned off a switch, it abruptly ends.

WHAT WE SO QUIETLY SAW.

by GREG COOK.

TEXT QUOTED DIRECTLY FROM FBI REPORTS ABOUT GUANTANAMO PRISONER INTERROGATIONS THAT WERE MADE PUBLIC IN RESPONSE TO A FREEDOM OF INFORMATION ACT REQUEST FILED BY THE AMERICAN CIVIL LIBERTIES UNION IN 2003.

"As requested here is a brief summary of what I observed at GITMO.

"On a couple of occasions, I entered interview rooms to find a detainee chained hand

"And foot in a fetal position to the floor, with no chair, food, or water.

"Most times they had urinated or defecated on themselves, and had been left there

"For 18, 24 hours or more. On one occasion, the air-conditioning had been turned down so far

"And the temperature was so cold in the room that the barefooted detainee was shaking with cold.

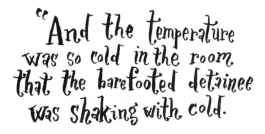

"When I asked the MP's what was going on, I was told that interrogators

"From the day prior had ordered this treatment, and the detainee was not to be moved.

"On another occasion the A/C had been turned off, making the temperature

"In the unventilated room probably well over 100 degrees.

"The detainee was almost unconscious on the floor, with a pile of hair next to him. He had apparently been

"Literally pulling his own hair out throughout the night.

"During late 2002, FBI Special Agent REDACTED was present in an observation room at GITMO and observed REDACTED (first name

"Unknown) REDACTED conducting an interrogation of an unknown detainee. ... REDACTED entered

"The observation room and complained that curtain movement at the observation window was distracting

"The detainee, although no movement of the curtain had occurred. She directed a marine

"To duct tape a curtain over the two-way mirror between the interrogation room and the observation room.

"SA REDACTED characterized this action as an attempt to prohibit those in the observation room from witnessing her interaction with the

"Detainee. Through the surveillance camera monitor SA REDACTED then observed REDACTED position herself between the detainee and the surveillance camera. The detainee was shackled

"And his hands were cuffed to his waist. SA REDACTED observed REDACTED apparently whispering

"In the detainee's ear, and caressing and applying lotion to his arms (this was during Ramadan when physical contact with

"A woman would have been particularly offensive to a Moslem male).

"On more than one occasion the detainee appeared to be grimacing in pain, and REDACTED's hands appeared to be making some contact with the detainee. Although SA REDACTED could not see

"Her hands at all times, he saw them moving towards the detainee's

"Lap. He also observed the detainee pulling away and against the restraints.

"Subsequently, the marine who had previously taped the curtain and had been in the interrogation room with REDACTED during the interrogation, re-entered

"The observation room. SA REDACTED asked what had happened to cause the detainee to grimace in pain. The marine said REDACTED had grabbed the

"Detainee's thumbs and bent them backwards and indicated that she also grabbed his genitals.

"A military interrogator and I were interviewing a new arrival at GITMO during the evening

"Hours when we heard what sounded like thunder. After hearing several 'thunderclaps'

"We stepped outside the interview room to take a break and see

"If the weather had made a drastic change from the clear skies we had witnessed prior to the start of our interview. As we walked down the hallway

"Of the temporary building where the interview rooms were located, I glanced in an open doorway where I saw at least two individuals dressed

"In BDU's [battle dress uniforms] standing and an inmate kneeling on the floor with his forehead on the ground. The inmate was

"Holding his nose and crying. There was a small amount of blood on the floor near the inmate's face. I asked the

"BDU-clad personnel what had happened. They explained that the inmate had become upset with them and threw himself to the floor...

"The inmate's nose appeared to be bleeding.

"One of the military personnel left the room to retrieve a medical kit

"For the inmate. I saw nothing

"To contradict the military personnel's explanation of events.

"While in Camp X-Ray, number REDACTED was aggressively interrogated by military reservists at the direction of REDACTED. During the interrogation, the reservists yelled and screamed at number REDACTED. Additionally, a

"German Shepard (sic) was positioned at the door to the interrogation

"Hut and made to growl and bark at the detainee.

"At one point, one of the interrogators placed a Koran in front of number REDACTED while number REDACTED was seated in a chair (apparently handcuffed to chair).

"The interrogator then straddled the Koran,

"At which point the detainee became very angry, but still

"Refused to provide any information.

"REDACTED and REDACTED were in an observation room, located

"Between two interrogation rooms, watching military personnel conduct an interrogation.

"At some point, REDACTED entered the room and told REDACTED to come with him as he wanted

"To show him something. REDACTED accompanied REDACTED to another observation room down the hall, where several

66

"Military Police were observing an interrogation. When he entered the observation room, REDACTED observed an unknown detainee with

"A full head of hair and a beard whose head was wrapped in duct tape in the adjacent interrogation room.

" There were two interrogators in the room with the detainee.

REDACTED asked REDACTED if the detainee had been spitting at the interrogators or exhibiting belligerent behavior toward them.

"REDACTED replied no, and then told REDACTED the detainee's head had been duct taped because he would not stop quoting the Koran.

"On several occasions when REDACTED questioned REDACTED about the techniques utilized, REDACTED said it had

"REDACTED did not approve of the treatment of the detainee and asked REDACTED how he planned to remove the duct tape, but REDACTED never answered him.

"Been approved by 'the Secretary' who REDACTED understood to be [Defense] Secretary [Donald] Rumsfeld.

"In November 2002, FBI agents observed Detainee REDACTED

"After he had been subjected to intense isolation over three months.

"During that time period REDACTED was totally isolated (with the exception of occasional interrogations)

"In a cell that was always flooded with light.

"By late November, the detainee was evidencing behavior consistent with extreme psychological trauma

"(Talking to non-existent people, reporting hearing voices, crouching in a corner of the cell covered

"With a sheet for hours on end). It is unknown to the FBI whether

"Such extended isolation was approved by appropriate DOD [Department of Defense] authorities."

THE MOSTLY BLACK NEIGHBORHOOD OF GREENWOOD WAS A CLASSIC AMERICAN SUCCESS STORY.

TULSA'S POPULATION EXPLODED AT THE TURN OF THE LAST CENTURY.

STOP WHERE YOU ARE!

NOBODY'S FIGHTING NO FIRES TONIGHT.

MANY RESIDENTS WERE FORMER SLAVES OR THEIR DESCENDENTS WHO'D TRAVELED WESTWARD ON THE TRAIL OF TEARS WITH EXILED AMERICAN INDIANS.

MOST CAME FOR THE PROMISES OF THE OIL BOOM.

"LIKE HELL I WILL"

BLACK TULSANS LARGELY WORKED HARD MANUAL LABOR AND SERVICE JOBS IN TOWN.

THE AFRICAN-AMERICAN COMMUNITY WAS THE BACKBONE OF TULSA'S PROSPERITY AFTER THE OIL DISCOVERIES OF 1905.

THIS NIGHT, THOUGH, NOBODY CARED ANYMORE ABOUT DICK ROWLAND AND THE CIRCUMSTANCES SURROUNDING HIS ELEVATOR RIDE.

THE CLOTHING STORE CLERK
SAID HE HEARD A WOMAN SCREAM.

DICK ROWLAND HAD JUST ENTERED
THE ELEVATOR IN THE BUILDING
DOWNTOWN WHERE HE SHINED SHOES.

THE ONLY WASHROOM HE WAS
ALLOWED TO USE WAS HIDDEN
AWAY ON THE EIGHTEENTH FLOOR.

DOWN THE STREET.

SARAH, A NINETEEN-YEAR-OLD WHITE
GIRL, OPERATED THE ELEVATOR
EACH DAY FOR DICK ROWLAND.

ON MAY 31ST, 1921, SOME SPECULATE
THAT HE TRIPPED AND GRABBED
SARAH'S ARM TO BREAK HIS FALL.

OTHERS SAY HE LIKELY
STEPPED ON HER FOOT.

GAVE HER A GOOD STARTLE.

NONE OF THAT MATTERED
WITHIN THE HOUR.

WE'LL NEVER KNOW WHAT SARAH
HAD TO SAY ABOUT IT ALL.
NO POLICE RECORDS REMAIN
OF HER STATEMENT.

A SEXUAL ASSAULT, SAYS THE CLERK.

"NAB NEGRO FOR ATTACKING GIRL IN ELEVATOR,"
SAYS THE FRONT PAGE OF THE NEWSPAPER.

THAT NIGHT, WHITE RIOTERS IMPRISONED BLACK RESIDENTS IN THEIR BURNING HOMES.

A MAN FLEEING THE BLAZE WAS SHOT TO DEATH. HIS CORPSE WAS THROWN BACK INTO THE FLAMES.

MUTILATED BODIES DRAGGED BEHIND AUTOS AND HORSES.

AMBULANCES WERE PREVENTED AT GUNPOINT FROM PICKING UP VICTIMS.

MOST LOCAL HOSPITALS WOULD NOT TREAT THEM ANYWAY.

AS GREENWOOD RESIDENTS SOUGHT SAFETY, SOME ORGANIZED, ARMING THEMSELVES IN DEFENSE OF THEIR NEIGHBORHOOD AND THOSE THEY LOVED.

DEFENDERS TOOK POSITION WITH RIFLES HIGH ATOP THE NEWLY DEDICATED MOUNT ZION CHURCH TOWER.

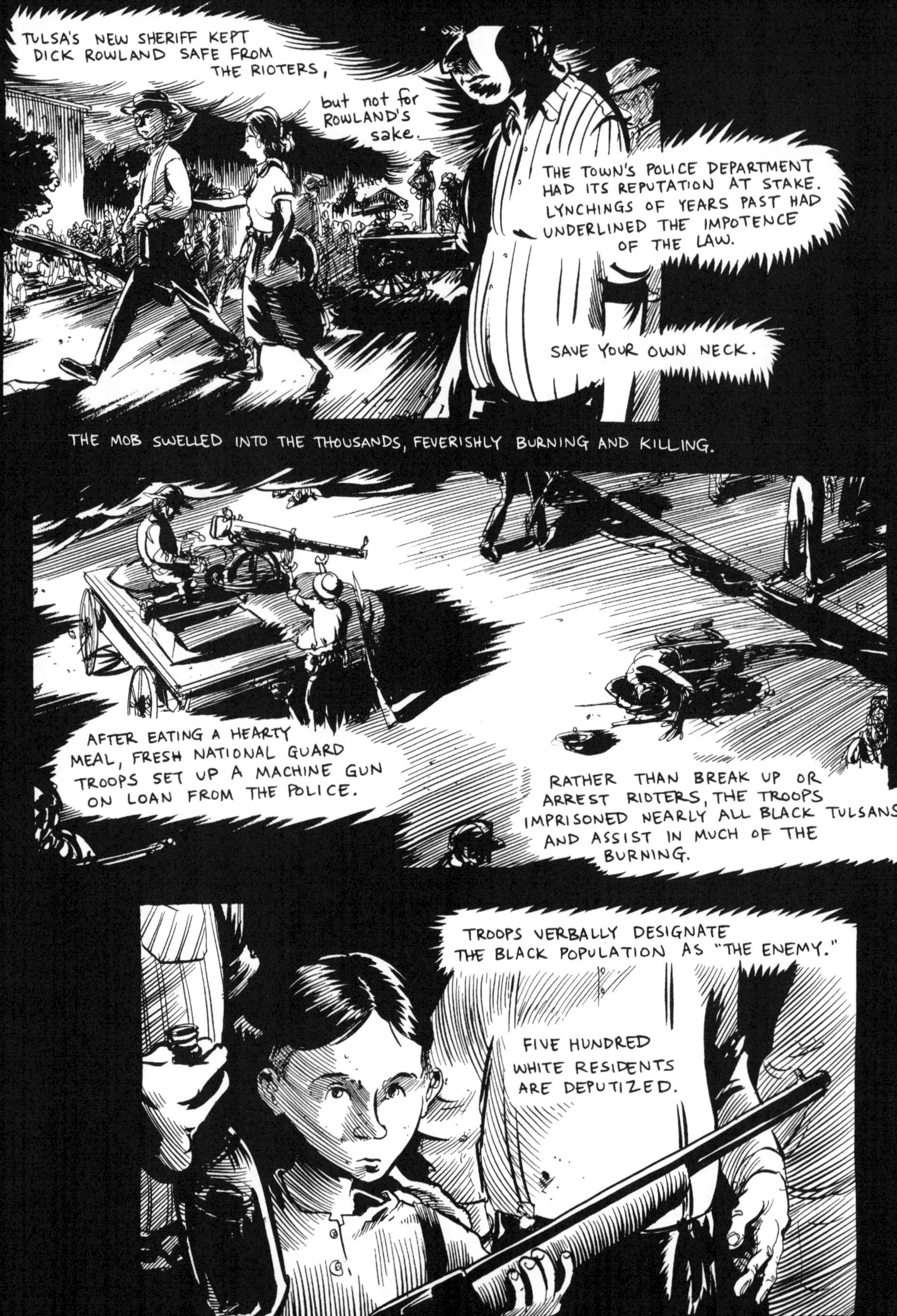
TULSA'S NEW SHERIFF KEPT DICK ROWLAND SAFE FROM THE RIOTERS,
but not for ROWLAND'S sake.
THE TOWN'S POLICE DEPARTMENT HAD ITS REPUTATION AT STAKE. LYNCHINGS OF YEARS PAST HAD UNDERLINED THE IMPOTENCE OF THE LAW.
SAVE YOUR OWN NECK.
THE MOB SWELLED INTO THE THOUSANDS, FEVERISHLY BURNING AND KILLING.
AFTER EATING A HEARTY MEAL, FRESH NATIONAL GUARD TROOPS SET UP A MACHINE GUN ON LOAN FROM THE POLICE.
RATHER THAN BREAK UP OR ARREST RIOTERS, THE TROOPS IMPRISONED NEARLY ALL BLACK TULSANS, AND ASSIST IN MUCH OF THE BURNING.
TROOPS VERBALLY DESIGNATE THE BLACK POPULATION AS "THE ENEMY."
FIVE HUNDRED WHITE RESIDENTS ARE DEPUTIZED.

SINCLAIR OIL LENDS OUT SEVERAL CURTISS JN-4 "JENNY" AIRPLANES TO THE ATTACKERS.

POLICE CAPTAIN G.H. BLAINE WAS ABOARD SEVERAL FLIGHTS, STRAFING BLACK RESIDENTS AS THEY FLED THE CITY.

MANY ACCOUNTS RECALL AIRBORNE FIREBOMBINGS, LIKELY TURPENTINE BOMBS.

MOUNT ZION CHURCH, JUST EIGHT WEEKS OLD, IS ONE OF SEVERAL DOZEN BUILDINGS BURNED TO THE GROUND.

MARY! LET ME IN!

SOME WHITE TULSANS DID SHELTER AND ASSIST THEIR BLACK NEIGHBORS.

through that door-- quick, now!

WHERE DID HE GO?!

where did WHO go?

DID YOU LET HIM IN HERE?!

mister, i'm not letting ANYBODY in here!

MARY JO ERHARDT HID A PURSUED CO-WORKER NAMED JACK IN THE BUILDING'S WALK-IN REFRIGERATOR AS SHE MISLED THE MOB.

IN HER AGE SHE RECALLED,

strangely, those guns frightened me not at all. i was so angry i could've torn those ruffians apart.

i cannot recall in all my life feeling hatred toward any person until then.

AS THE SUN CLIMBED, RIOTERS BECAME SLEEP-DEPRIVED AND FATIGUED.

MANY WHITE STUDENTS SKIPPED SCHOOL TO PARTICIPATE IN THE MASSACRE.

YOU CAN _HAVE_ IT.

I'M GOING TO _BED._

THE DEATH TOLL VARIES FROM 300 TO 3,000 OR MORE, LIKELY THE LATTER BASED ON THE SHEER NUMBER OF GRAVE-DIGGING TEAMS.

MOST OF THE VICTIMS WERE BURIED IN SHALLOW, UNMARKED, OR MASS GRAVES OUTSIDE TOWN.

MOST HAD NO FAMILY PRESENT AT THEIR BURIALS, AS NEARLY ALL BLACK TULSANS WERE IMPRISONED FOR THE NEXT WEEK.

MANY SURVIVORS NEVER LEARNED WHERE LOVED ONES WERE BURIED.

NO WHITE TULSAN WAS <u>EVER</u> IMPRISONED FOR THE MASSACRE.

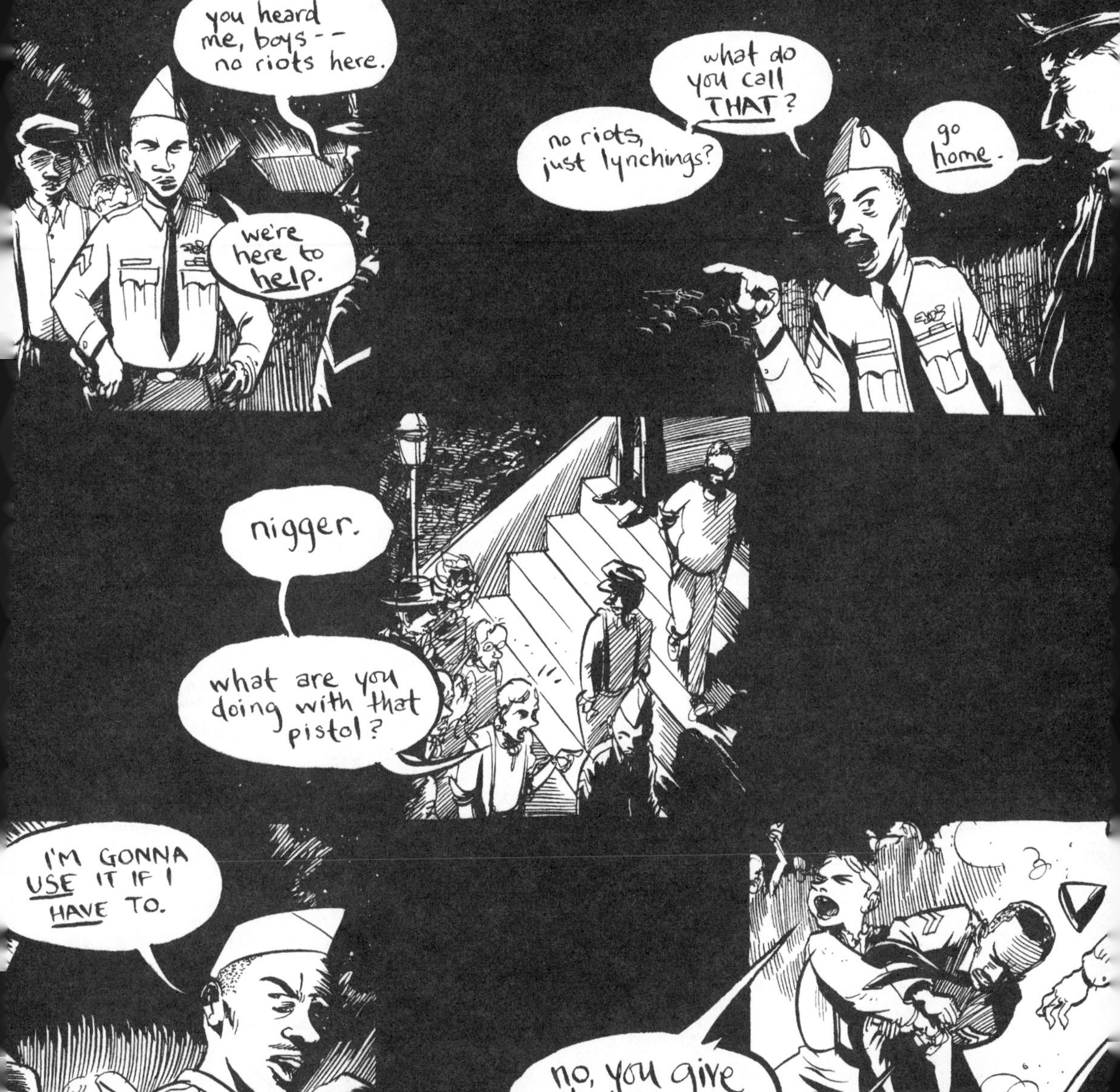
you heard me, boys -- no riots here.
we're here to help.
what do you call THAT?
no riots, just lynchings?
go home.
nigger.
what are you doing with that pistol?
I'M GONNA USE IT IF I HAVE TO.
no, you give it to me!
LIKE HELL I WILL.

Welcome home, brave

NO MATTER WHERE YOU LIVE, INDIANS LIVED THERE BEFORE YOU.

WE WERE THE FIRST AMERICANS.

YOU GAVE US THE NAME, BUT WE HAD MANY BEFORE THAT.

A NAME THAT STUCK TO US BECAUSE OF YOUR NAVIGATIONAL ERROR.

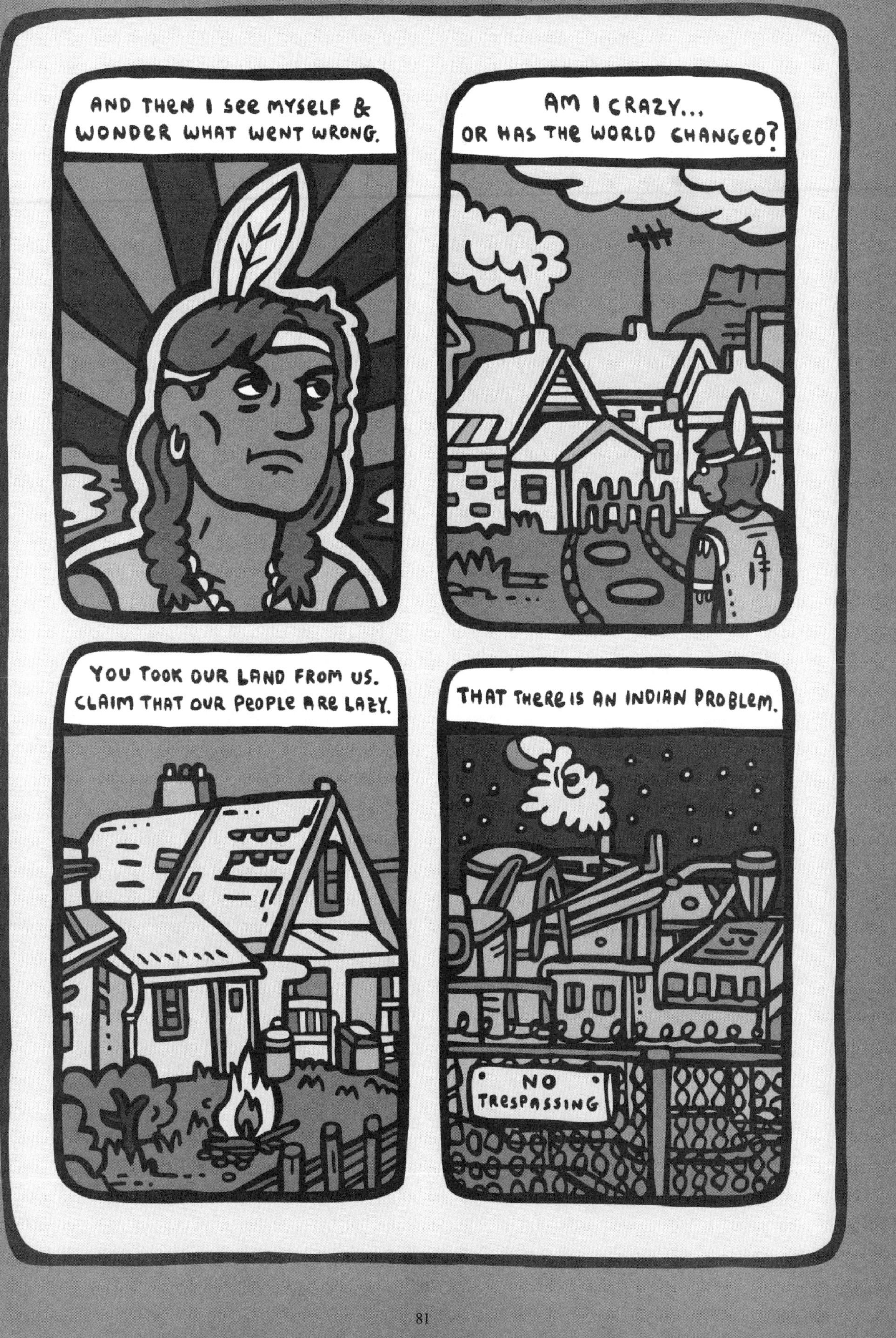
AND THEN I SEE MYSELF & WONDER WHAT WENT WRONG.
AM I CRAZY... OR HAS THE WORLD CHANGED?
YOU TOOK OUR LAND FROM US. CLAIM THAT OUR PEOPLE ARE LAZY.
THAT THERE IS AN INDIAN PROBLEM.
NO TRESPASSING

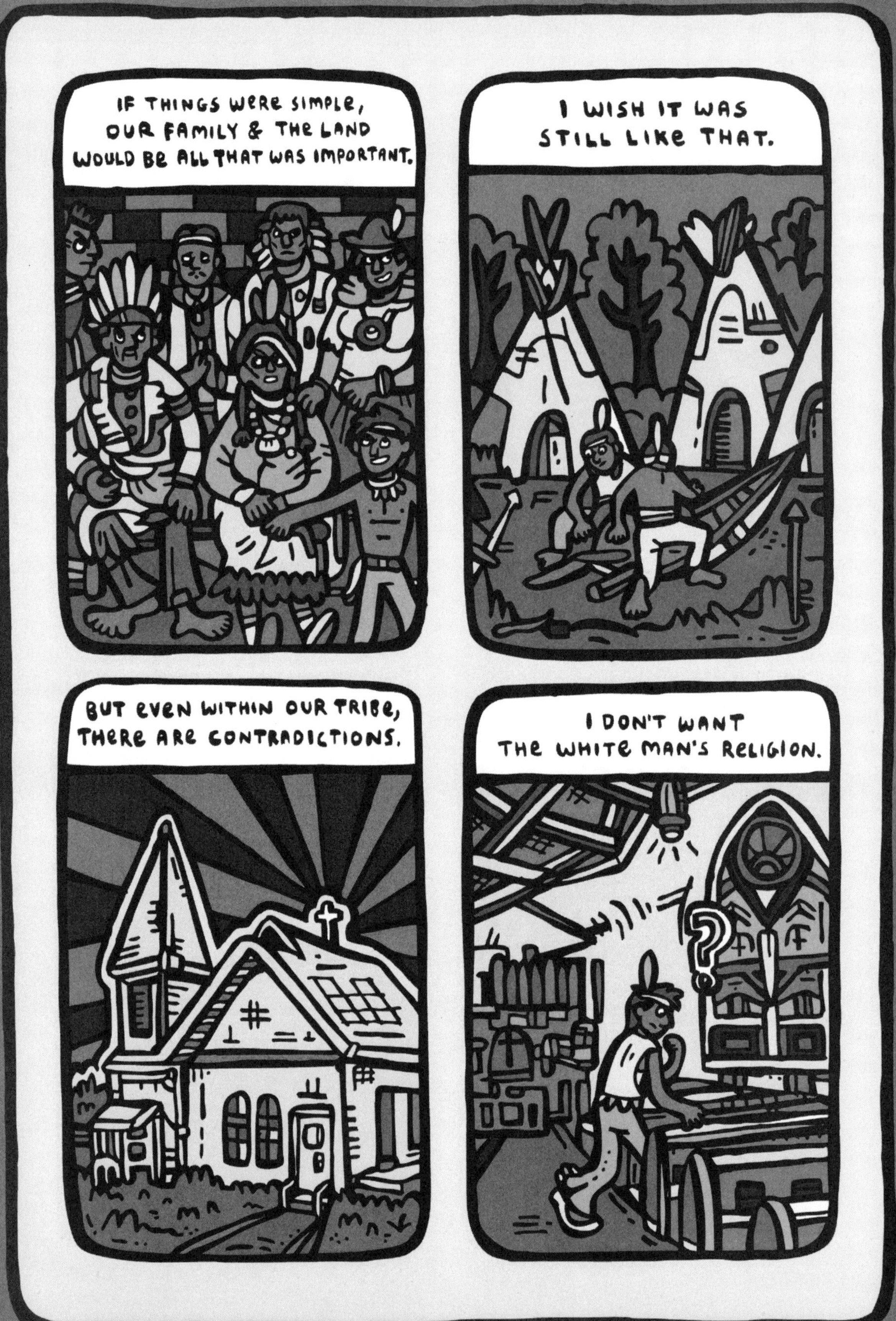
IF THINGS WERE SIMPLE, OUR FAMILY & THE LAND WOULD BE ALL THAT WAS IMPORTANT.
I WISH IT WAS STILL LIKE THAT.
BUT EVEN WITHIN OUR TRIBE, THERE ARE CONTRADICTIONS.
I DON'T WANT THE WHITE MAN'S RELIGION.

MY FAMILY IS NOT WITHOUT MONEY.

DAD OWNS A SHOP THAT SELLS TRINKETS.

FOR TOURISTS.

SOMEHOW, I WANT MORE.

I WANT TO BE WILD,

TO STAND ON MY HEAD,

TO TAKE MY PANTS OFF,

TO JOIN THE CIRCUS
...THIS IS WHO I AM,

CAN YOU LOVE ME
FOR THAT?

OR AM I OFF MY ROCKER?

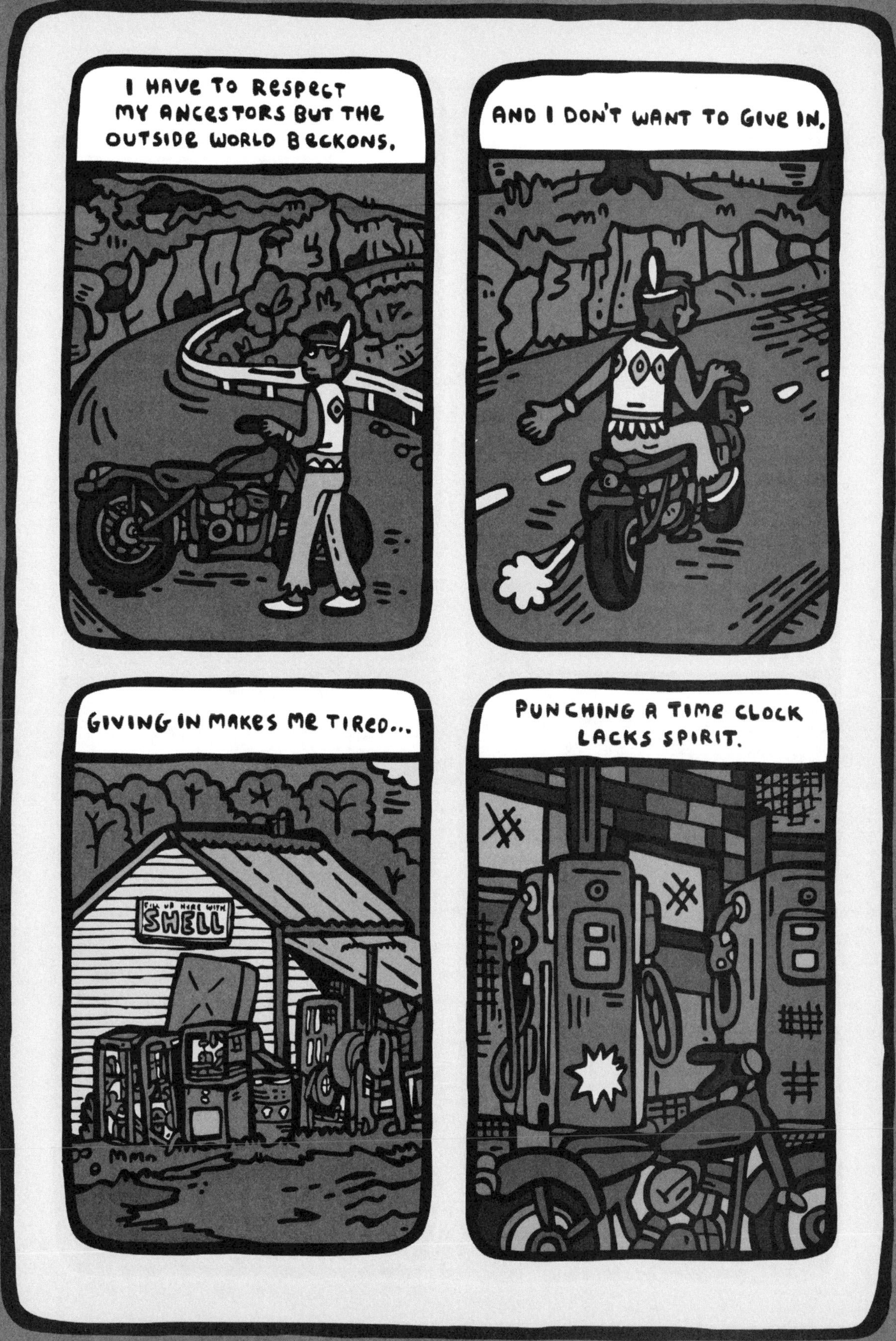
I HAVE TO RESPECT MY ANCESTORS BUT THE OUTSIDE WORLD BECKONS.
AND I DON'T WANT TO GIVE IN.
GIVING IN MAKES ME TIRED...
FILL UP HERE WITH SHELL
PUNCHING A TIME CLOCK LACKS SPIRIT.

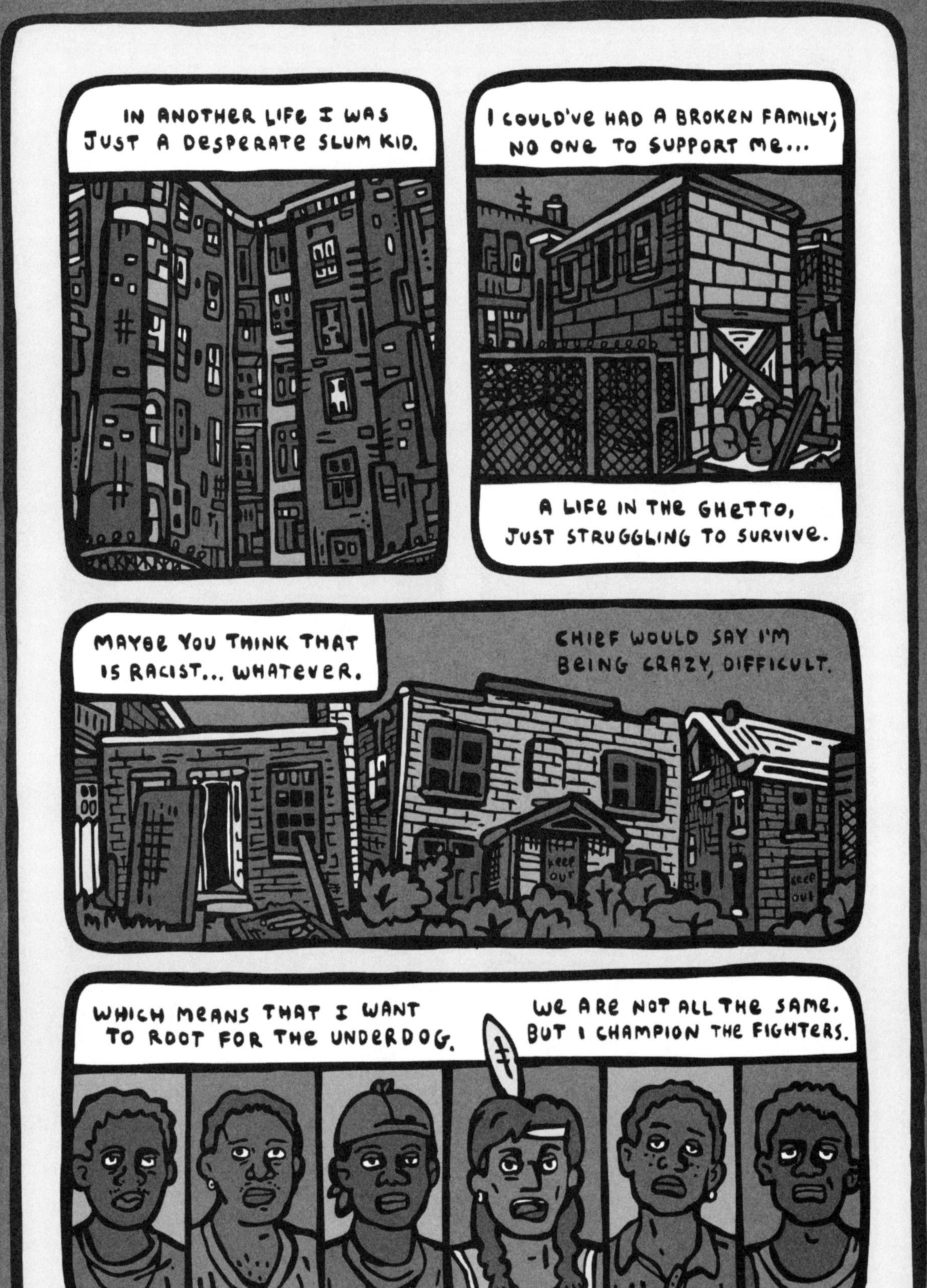
IN ANOTHER LIFE I WAS JUST A DESPERATE SLUM KID.
I COULD'VE HAD A BROKEN FAMILY; NO ONE TO SUPPORT ME...
A LIFE IN THE GHETTO, JUST STRUGGLING TO SURVIVE.
MAYBE YOU THINK THAT IS RACIST... WHATEVER.
CHIEF WOULD SAY I'M BEING CRAZY, DIFFICULT.
KEEP OUT
KEEP OUT
WHICH MEANS THAT I WANT TO ROOT FOR THE UNDERDOG.
WE ARE NOT ALL THE SAME. BUT I CHAMPION THE FIGHTERS.

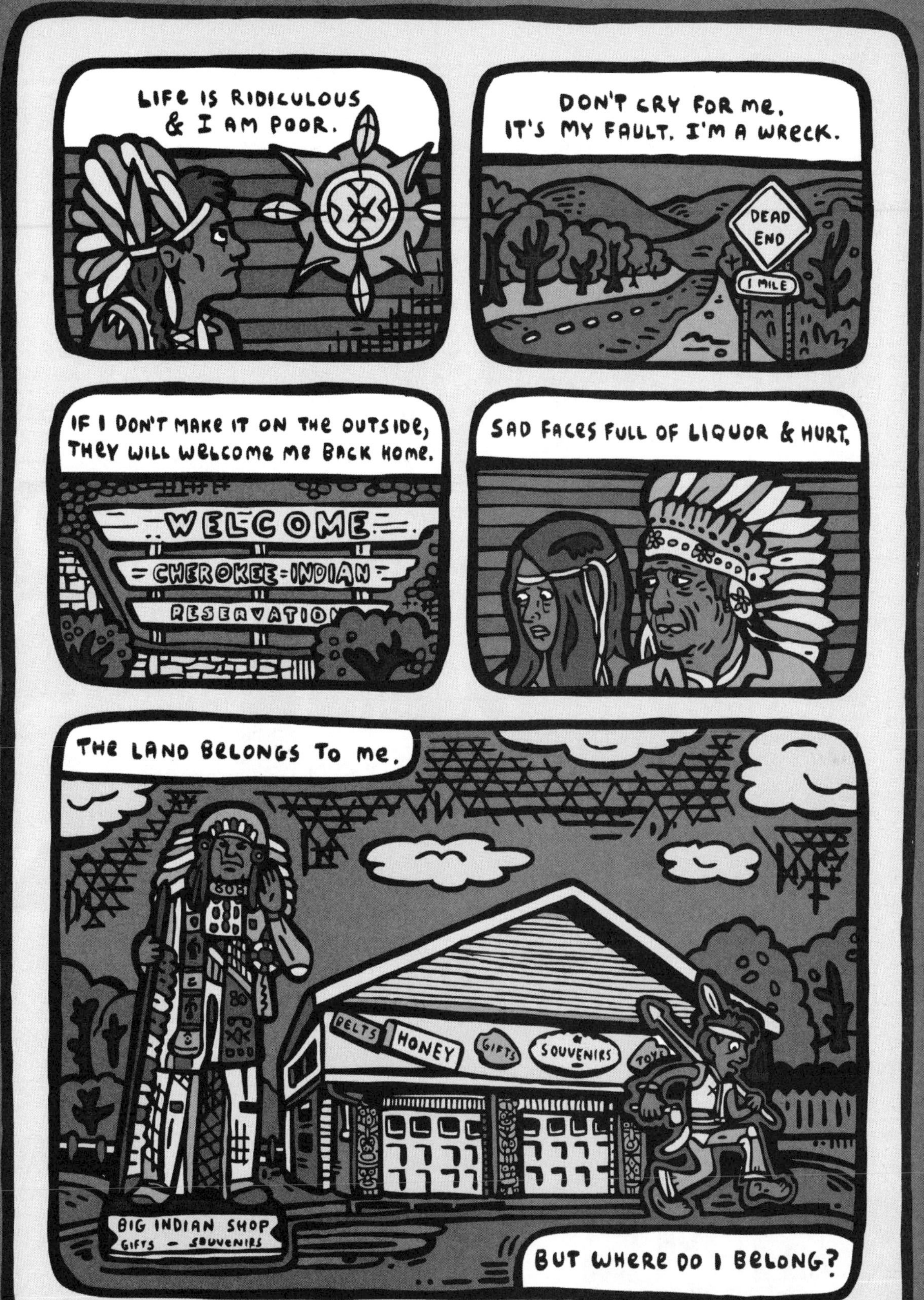
LIFE IS RIDICULOUS & I AM POOR.
DON'T CRY FOR ME. IT'S MY FAULT. I'M A WRECK.
DEAD END
1 MILE
IF I DON'T MAKE IT ON THE OUTSIDE, THEY WILL WELCOME ME BACK HOME.
WELCOME
CHEROKEE INDIAN
RESERVATION
SAD FACES FULL OF LIQUOR & HURT.
THE LAND BELONGS TO ME.
BELTS
HONEY
GIFTS
SOUVENIRS
BIG INDIAN SHOP
GIFTS - SOUVENIRS
BUT WHERE DO I BELONG?
XXX BRAVE K.

THE SOUND OF JADE

HEY DAD, LOOK!

WOW, I GUESS THAT'S GOING TO BE US IN A FEW HOURS.

ARE YOU NERVOUS?

YOU COULD DEFINITELY SAY THAT!

HOLLY AND I HAVE WAITED SO LONG FOR THIS... AND NOW IT'S ACTUALLY HAPPENING.

WE SHOULD PUT THESE ON, SO SHE'LL KNOW WHO WE ARE.

RANDALL GLIDDEN 格而也 (Mei Li Long)

SARAH GLIDDEN (sister) 格 而 也 Long

HA HA.

MY DAD AND I WERE IN WUHAN, CHINA, WITH FIVE OTHER FAMILIES GROUPED TOGETHER BY THE CHILDREN'S HOME SOCIETY OF MINNEAPOLIS, AN INTERNATIONAL ADOPTION AGENCY.

IN 2004, AMERICANS ADOPTED 7,044 BABIES FROM CHINA. SIX OF THEM WOULD BE GOING BACK TO THE U.S. WITH OUR GROUP.

BEFORE ADOPTION DAY, THE AGENCY SET UP TOURS IN BEIJING SO WE COULD GET MORE FAMILIAR WITH THE COUNTRY AND EACH OTHER.

THERE WERE THE MOIS, ABOUT TO ADOPT THEIR SECOND DAUGHTER...

ISN'T THIS EXCITING JENNY? YOU GET TO SEE WHERE YOU CAME FROM!

YEAH.

AND JANE, A SINGLE MOTHER-TO-BE, WHO BROUGHT HER FRIEND ANNETTE ALONG FOR MORAL SUPPORT.

I'VE JUST ALWAYS KNOWN I WAS MEANT TO BE A MOTHER.

THE DICKERSONS, THE FOLEYS AND THE DAMBRINIS HAD ALSO GONE THROUGH A YEAR'S WORTH OF INTERVIEWS, HOME VISITS AND PAPERWORK TO GET HERE.

INCREDIBLE!

AND THEN THERE WAS MY DAD, WHO AT THE AGE OF 54 WAS ABOUT TO ADD A NEW DAUGHTER TO HIS SECOND FAMILY.

CAN I SEE THE PHOTO OF LI-LONG AGAIN?

SURE!

MY STEPMOTHER DECIDED TO STAY HOME WITH THEIR THREE-YEAR-OLD (MY HALF-SISTER) SO I CAME ALONG TO HELP OUT.

IN 2006, THE CHINA CENTER FOR ADOPTION AFFAIRS WOULD TIGHTEN RESTRICTIONS FOR PROSPECTIVE PARENTS.

PEOPLE WHO ARE SINGLE, OVERWEIGHT OR OVER THE AGE OF 50 WOULD NO LONGER BE ELIGIBLE.

THAT WOULD HAVE EXCLUDED MANY PEOPLE IN OUR GROUP INCLUDING MY FATHER.

BUT IT WAS 2004, WHICH MEANT THAT WITHIN AN HOUR EVERYONE ON OUR BUS WOULD BE A NEW MOM OR DAD...

OOH! WE'RE HERE!

EXCEPT JENNY AND ME.

SO IT LOOKS LIKE WE'RE GONNA BE BIG SISTERS. PRETTY COOL, HUH?

I GUESS.

OUR GUIDE AND TRANSLATOR SAID HER NAME WAS CATHY. MOST CHINESE SEEM TO ADOPT WESTERN SOUNDING NAMES FOR DEALING WITH AMERICANS.

WE WILL GO TO THE SIXTH FLOOR FOR YOUR BABIES.

I SUPPOSE THIS IS SO WE DON'T HAVE TO FURTHER EMBARRASS OURSELVES. IT'S DIFFICULT ENOUGH TO SAY "THANK YOU."

XEI XEI.

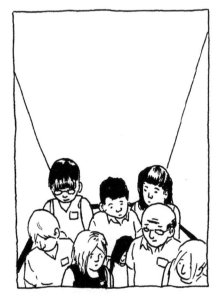

DING!
HERE WE ARE!

PLEASE, THIS WAY.

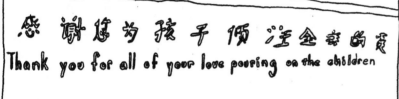

CATHY TRANSLATED FOR A GOVERNMENT OFFICIAL WHO TOLD US WE WOULD BE TAKING THE BABIES BACK TO THE HOTEL FOR A 24-HOUR DECIDING PERIOD.

SO IF YOU GET THE BABY AND YOU WANT TO ADOPT HER, WE WILL COME BACK HERE TOMORROW MORNING.

YOUR MOM AND I DIDN'T HAVE THE OPTION TO RETURN YOU TO THE HOSPITAL!

DAD!

PLEASE STEP FORWARD FOR YOUR BABY WHEN I CALL YOUR NAME.

THERE WAS NO NEED FOR NAMES. ALL THE PARENTS KNEW THEIR DAUGHTERS BY SIGHT AFTER SPENDING SIX MONTHS LOOKING AT THEIR PHOTOS.

OH!

OOO OHH!

WAAAAAAAAAA! AAA!

IT'S REALLY A BABY!

WAH! AAAA! AAA! AAAA!

AAYAAAA!

WAAAAAA! YAAAAAA!

NO ONE CAN PREDICT WHAT IT WILL BE LIKE THE MOMENT THEY MEET THEIR CHILD, ADOPTED OR OTHERWISE...

AAAA! AAAA! AA

SHHHH...

BUT I DOUBT THAT ANYONE IMAGINES SO MUCH CRYING DURING THE HAPPY EVENT.

RANDALL GLIDDEN!

WAHH! A VAHH!

IT'S HER!

92

HI!

AaaaAAAAAaa!

WAAA! WAWAAAH!

AWW!

WAAH! WAAWAWAAA! MAHAAAAH!

AAAAAAAAA!

YAAA! WAYAAAAAAA,

MAYBE WE SHOULD SIT DOWN.

SHHH! DON'T CRY!

WE GOT A BAG OF STUFF FROM THE ORPHANAGE. MAYBE THERE'S A PACIFIER INSIDE.

AAAAAAAA, AAAAA

THAT MUST BE WHAT SHE WAS FOUND IN.

IT WAS JUST A LITTLE WHITE SHIRT WITH A NOTE PINNED TO IT STATING HER BIRTHDAY.

IT WAS THE ORPHANAGE THAT GAVE HER THE NAME 'MEI LI LONG.' 'MEI' FOR THE PROVINCE. 'LONG' MEANS 'THE SOUND OF JADE.'

ALL SIX GIRLS HAD BEEN GIVEN THE MIDDLE NAME 'LI' MEANING BEAUTIFUL.

THE 'LI SISTERS' HAD ALL COME TO WUHAN THAT MORNING ON A FOUR HOUR BUS RIDE.

SHE'S TOO LOUD!

AAAIAAA!

PRIOR TO THAT DAY, THEY HAD BEEN LIVING WITH FOSTER FAMILIES WHILE THEIR ADOPTIONS WERE BEING PROCESSED.

AAH..MRGG...

PHOTOS!

THOSE MUST BE FROM THE DISPOSABLE CAMERA THE AGENCY HAD US SEND TO THE FOSTER PARENTS.

SNIFF.

IN ONE ROOM, IN FIVE MINUTES, TEN PEOPLE SIMULTANEOUSLY BECAME PARENTS.

THEIR SHARED PREGNANCY ENDED ABRUPTLY.

I NEED TO BUY FORMULA AND SIGN SOME PAPERS. CAN YOU WATCH HER?

OF COURSE!

LI LONG WAS 14 MONTHS OLD WHEN WE TOOK HER HOME, OLD ENOUGH TO REMEMBER THE PEOPLE SHE HAD JUST BEEN SEPARATED FROM.

AFTER NAPPING BRIEFLY, SHE WOKE UP AND BEGAN WAILING AND POINTING OUT THE WINDOW.

AAAAAH! AAAA!

THIS LASTED ALMOST AN HOUR. SHE EVEN TRIED TO OPEN IT AND CLIMB OUT.

AAAAA!

OH, NO YOU DON'T!

I'D NEVER HEARD A BABY CRY LIKE THAT. IT WASN'T A CRY OF DISCOMFORT HUNGER OR PHYSICAL PAIN, BUT ONE OF LOSS.

AAAₐₐₐAAAA!

MY DAD MISSED THE WHOLE THING, WHICH WAS PROBABLY FOR THE BEST.

I'M BACK! HOW ARE MY DAUGHTERS?

GREAT!

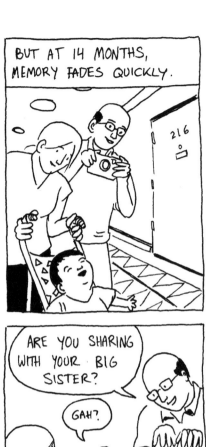

BUT AT 14 MONTHS, MEMORY FADES QUICKLY.

BY THE NEXT DAY SHE SEEMED TO HAVE FORGOTTEN THE TRAUMA OF THE ADOPTION DAY.

WHO'S GOT A SNACK?

HER NEW NAME WAS ANNE.

OH, WHY THANK YOU!

ARE YOU SHARING WITH YOUR BIG SISTER?

GAH?

WELL, I HAVE A BOTTLE JUST FOR YOU.

HERE, ANNE, LUNCHTIME!

THE END

SUBWAY BUSKERS

DRAWN BY VICTOR MARCHAND KERLOW

THE FOLLOWING DRAWINGS WERE ALL DONE ON LOCATION IN THE SUBWAY SYSTEMS OF NEW YORK. DOING THIS SERIES ON LOCATION MEANT RUNNING UP AND DOWN STAIRCASES, THROUGH PASSAGEWAYS, AROUND CROWDS OF HUMAN TRAFFIC, LISTENING FOR MUSIC ABOVE THE MORE COMMON SOUNDS OF A TRAIN STATION. SOME DRAWINGS WERE DONE DURING RUSH HOUR, OTHERS LATER IN THE EVENING, AND A COUPLE DONE IN THE EARLY HOURS OF THE MORNING. MOST OF THE MUSICIANS WHO PERFORM IN THE SUBWAYS OF NEW YORK ARE FAMILIAR WITH ONE ANOTHER, SO DURING THE COURSE OF DRAWING ONE PERSON, OTHERS I HAD PREVIOUSLY DRAWN WOULD COME UP IN CONVERSATION, AS WELL AS A FEW I WOULD GO ON TO DRAW LATER.

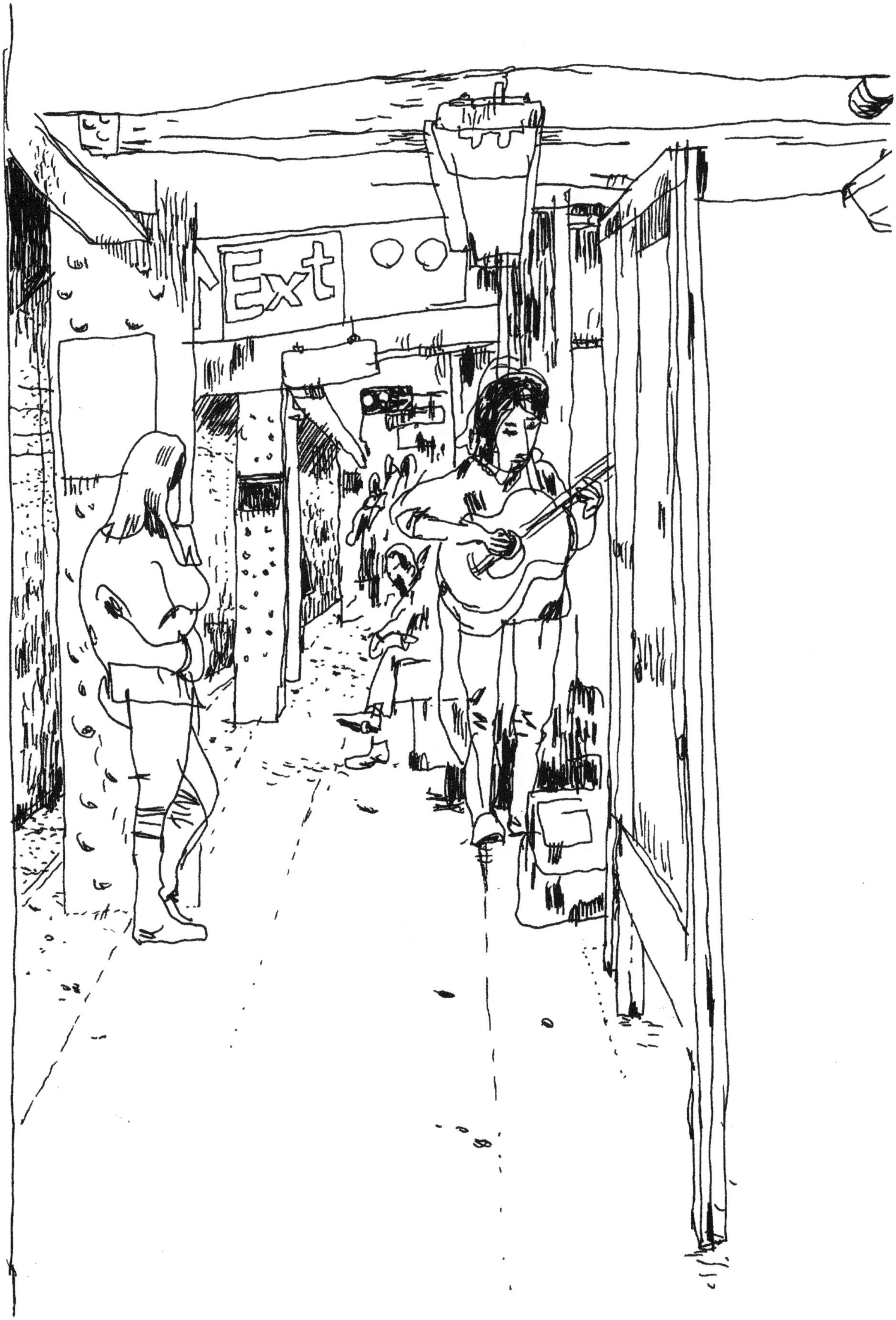
Ext

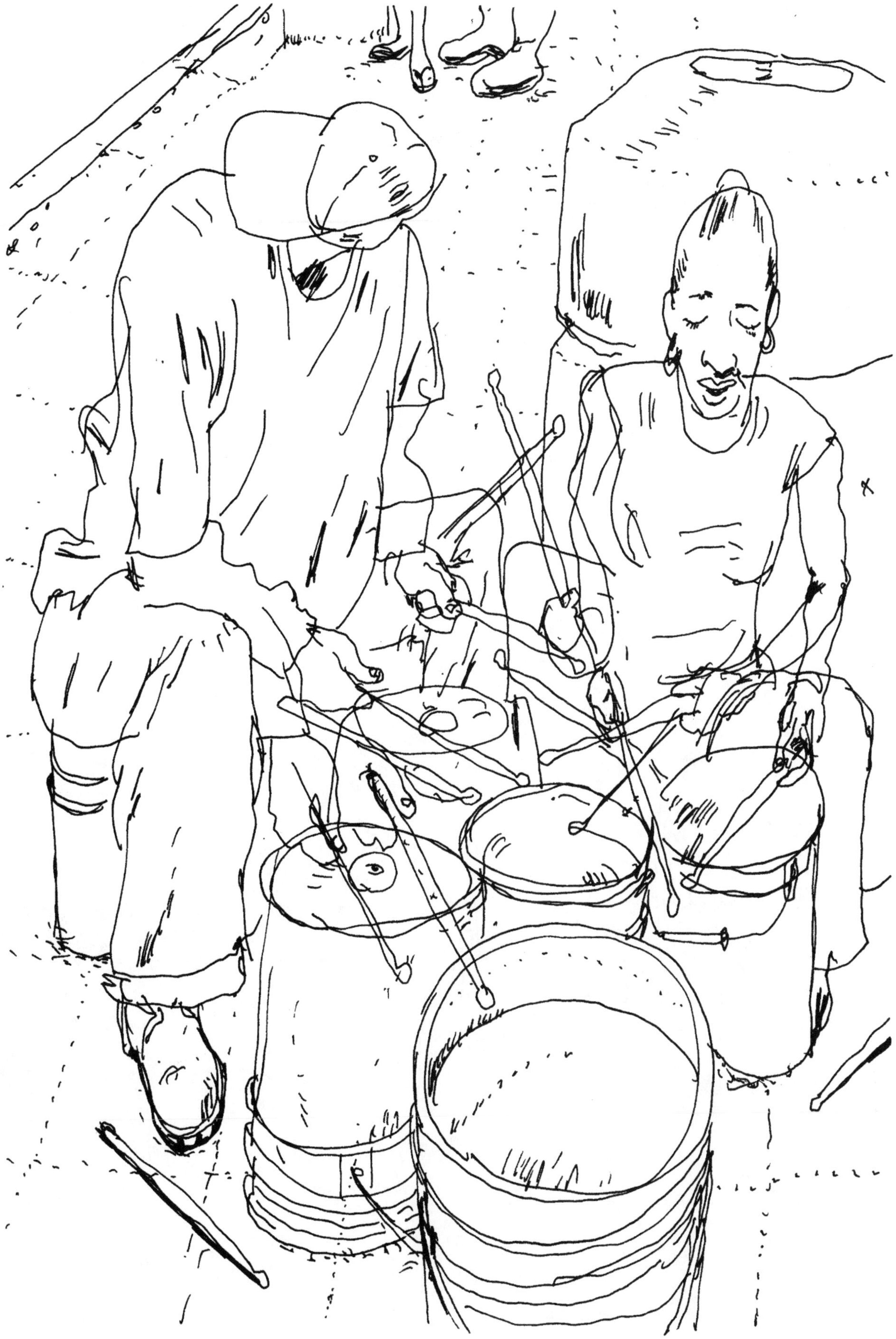

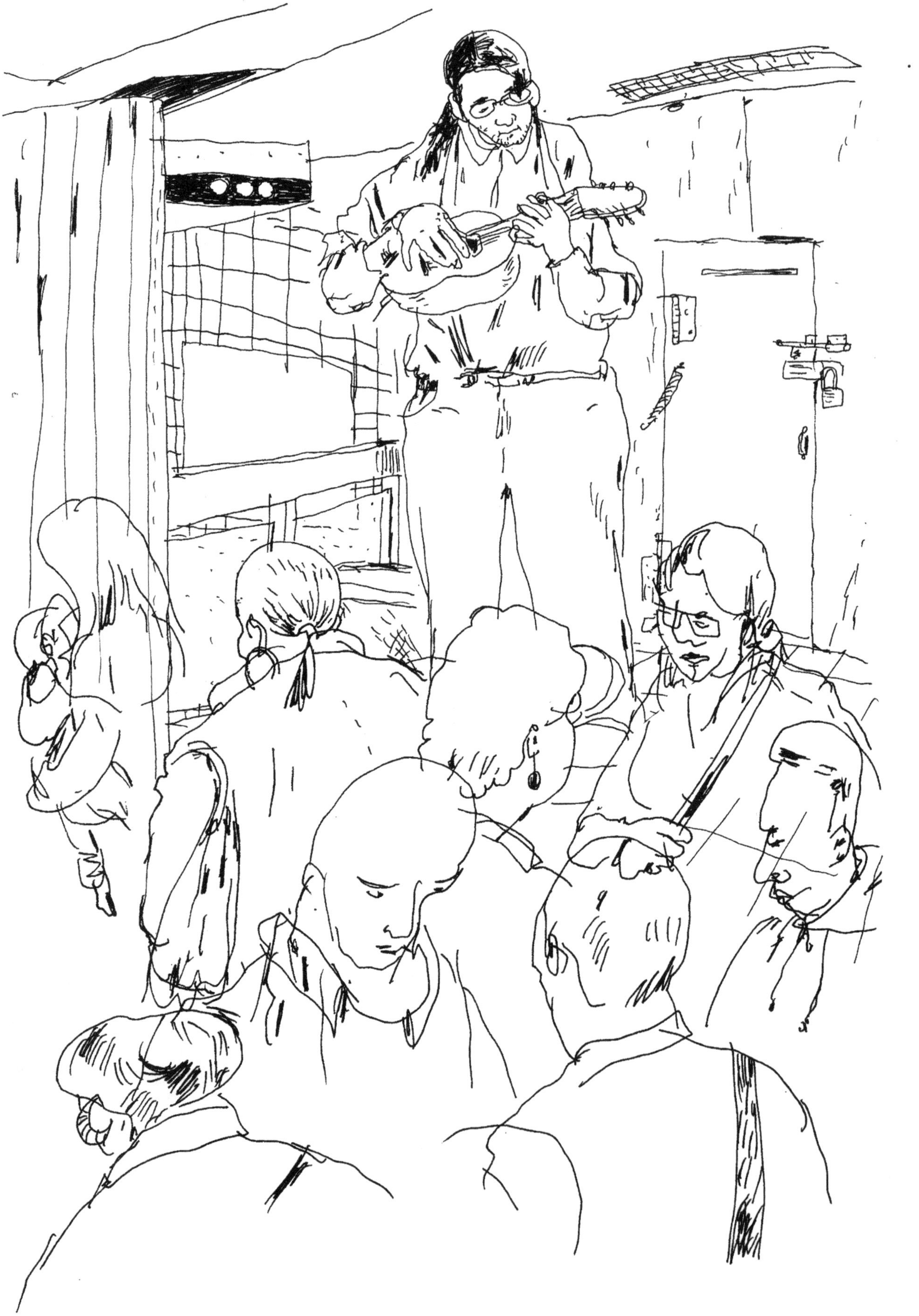

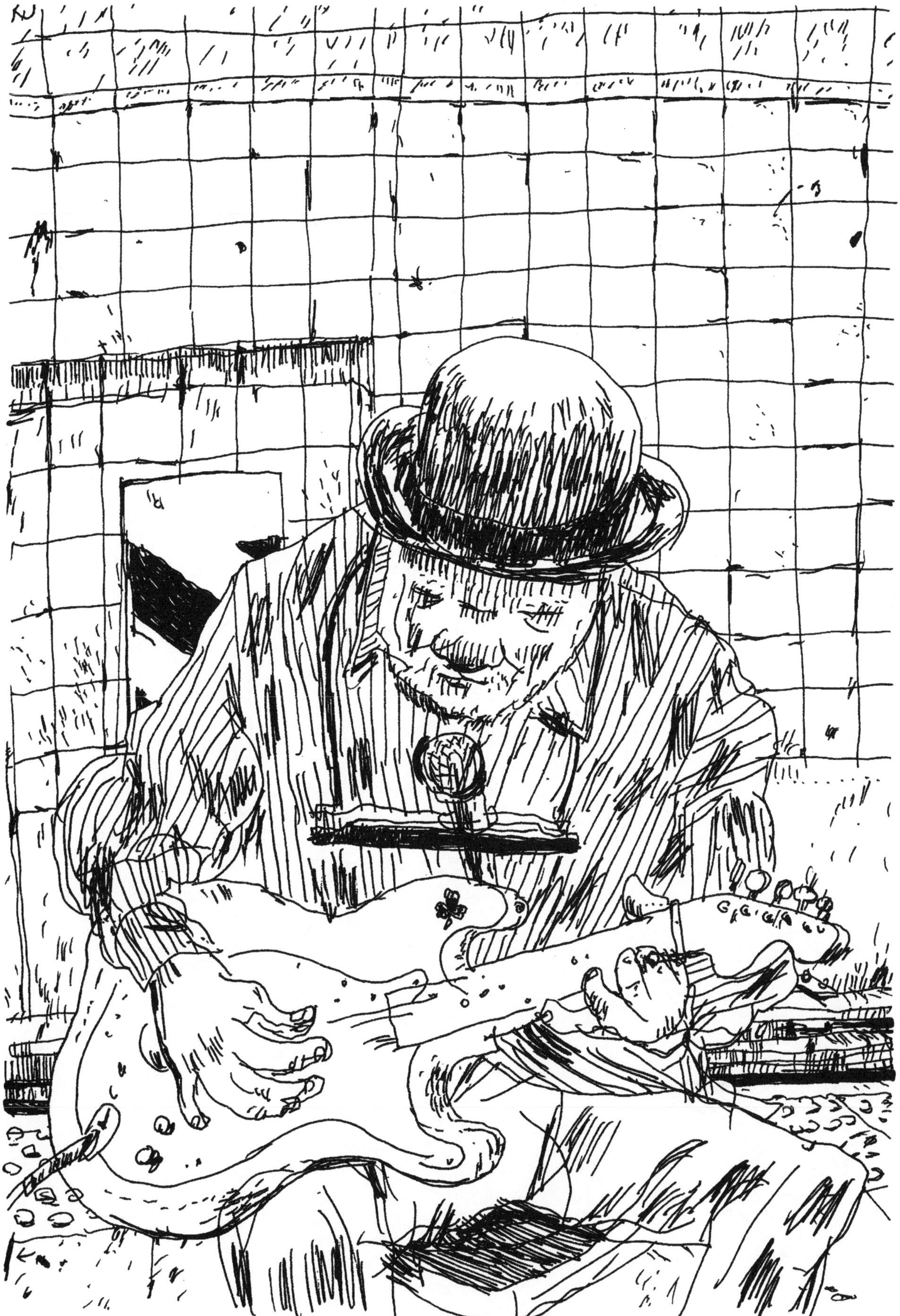

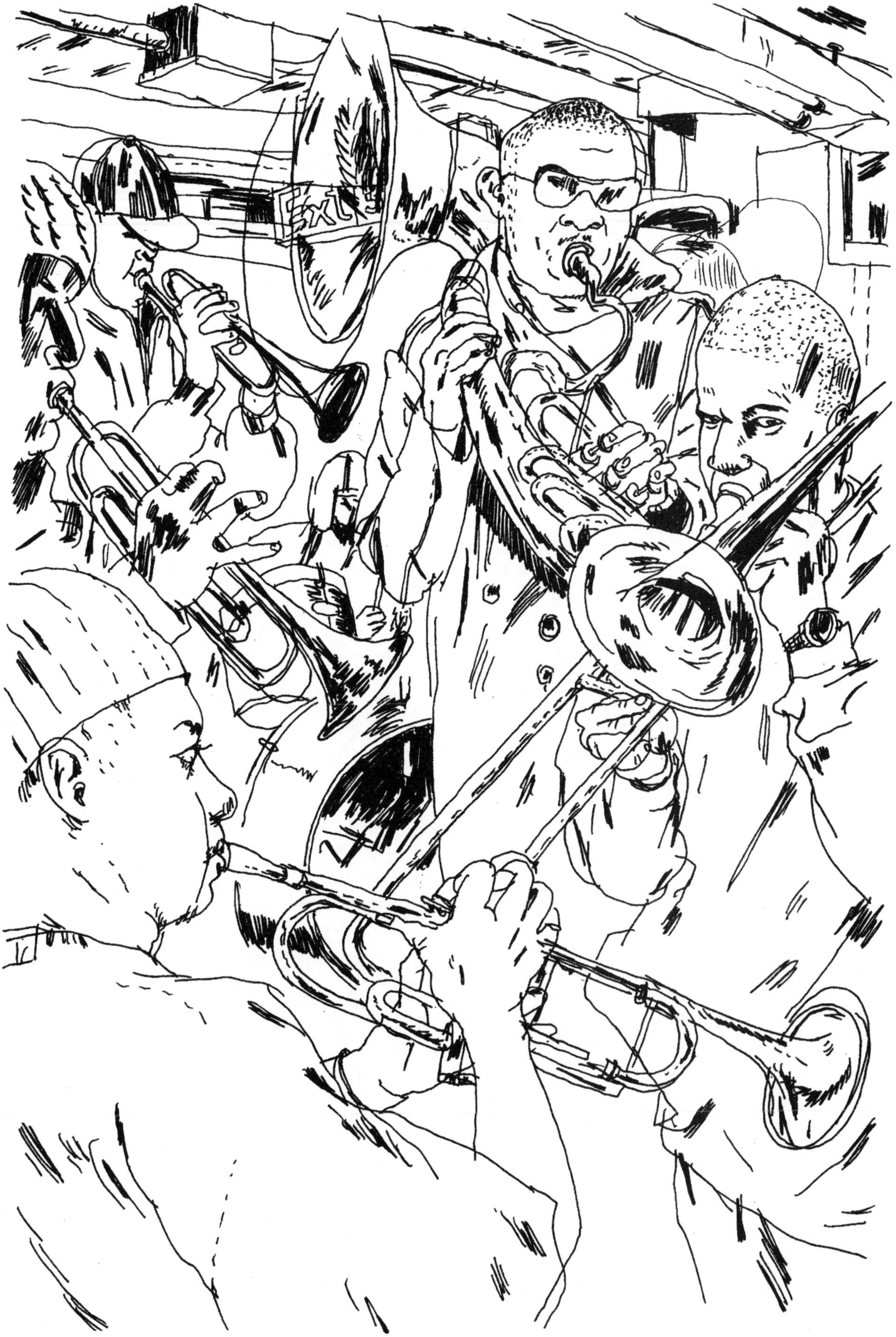

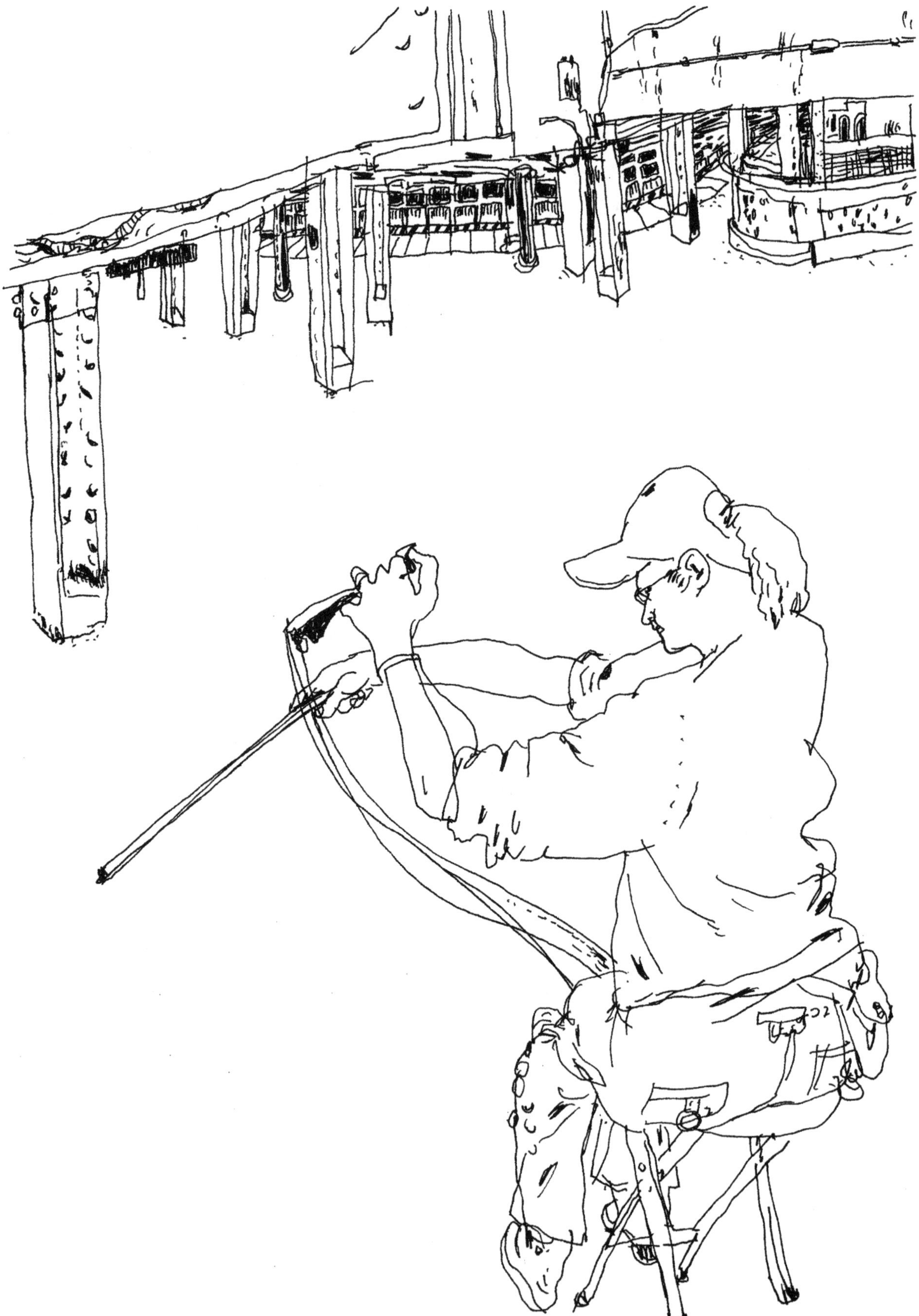

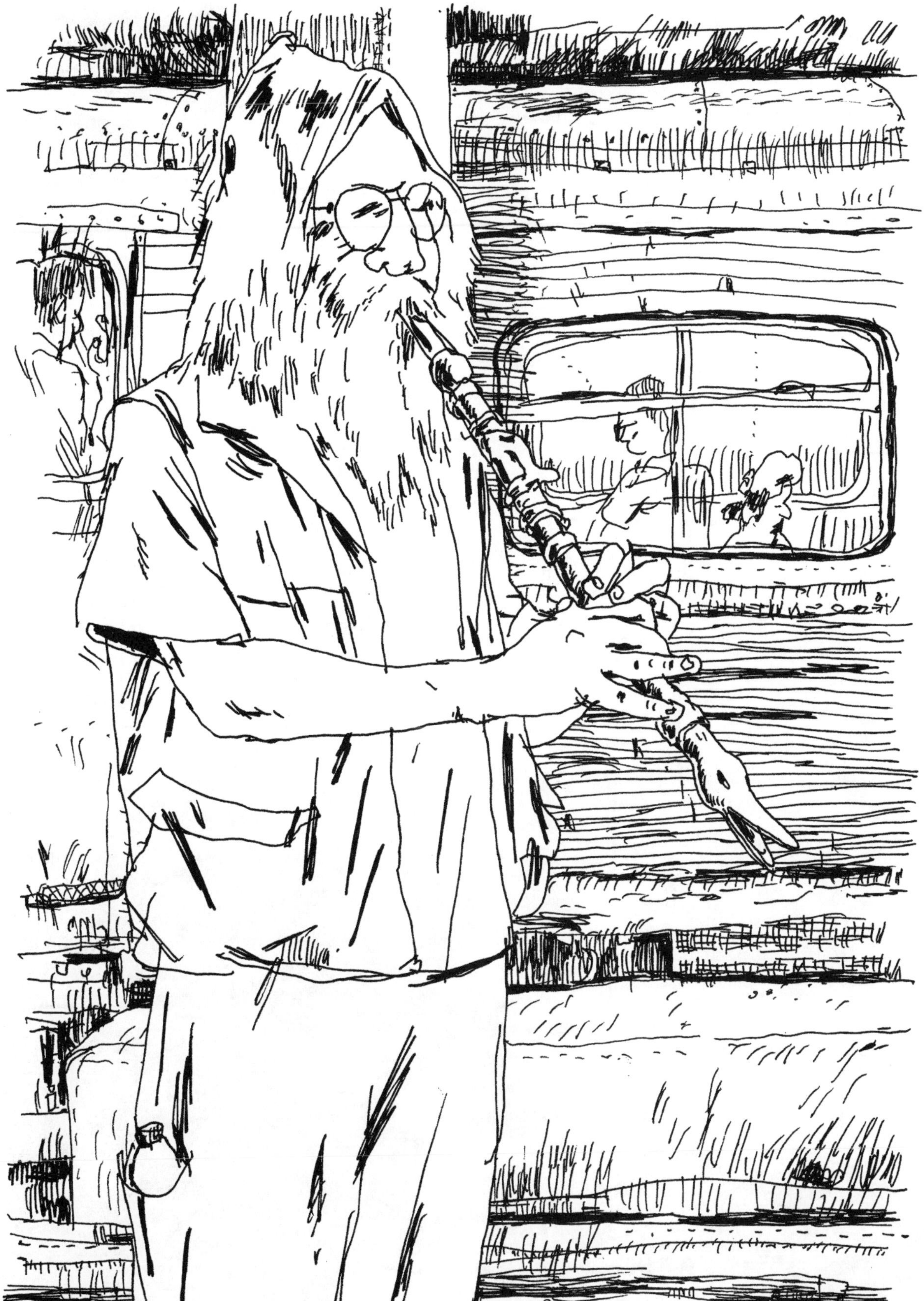

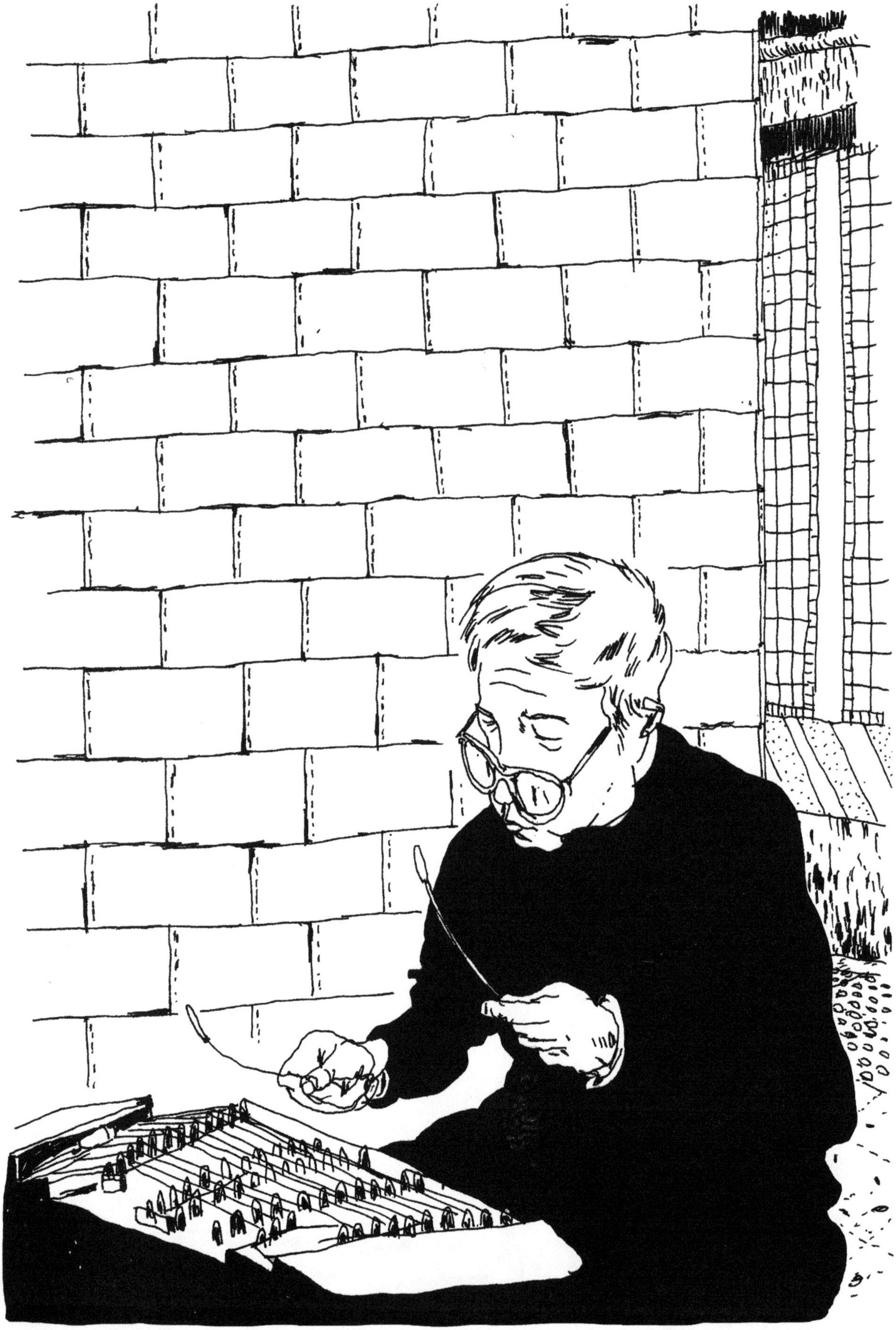

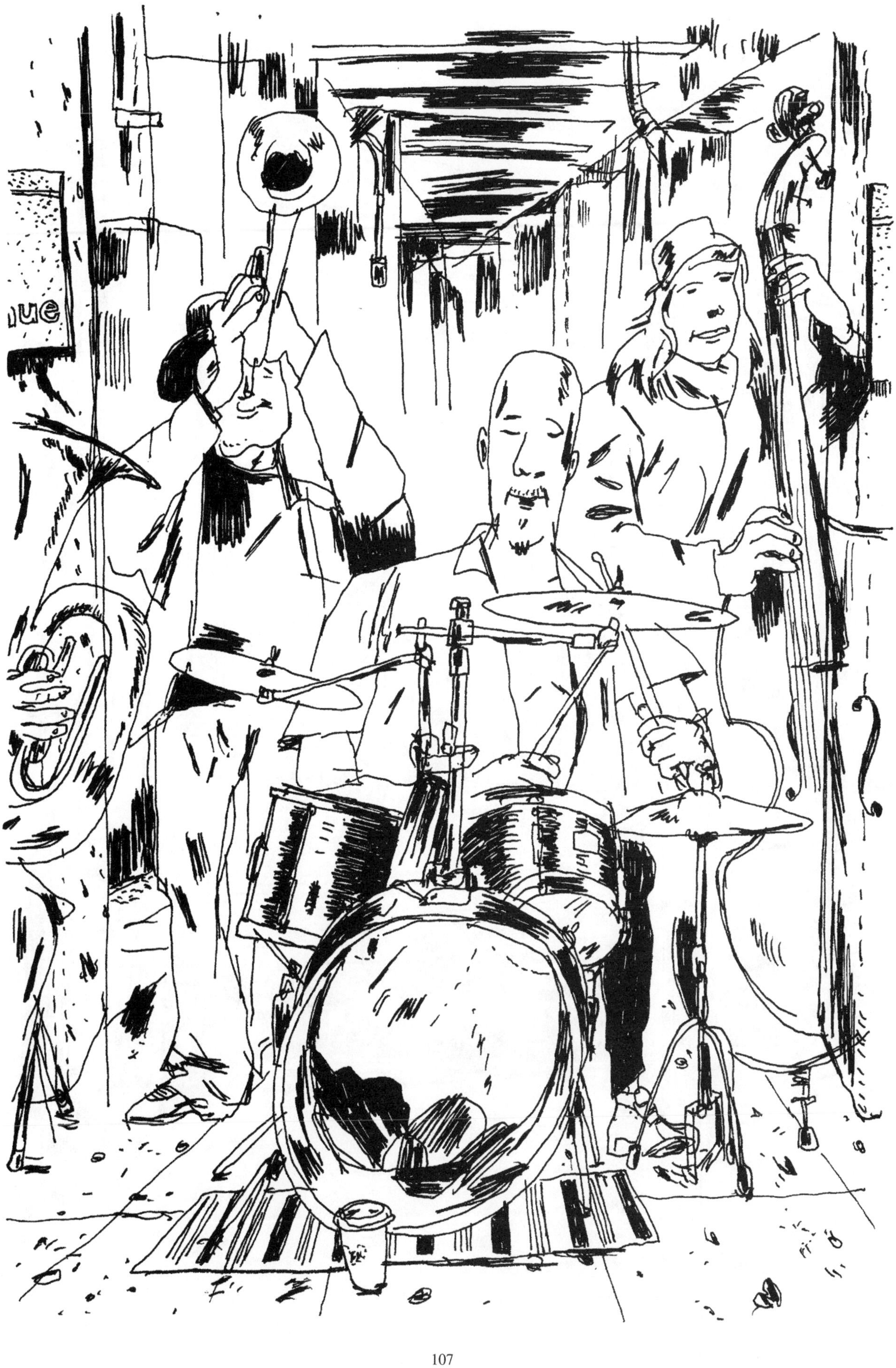

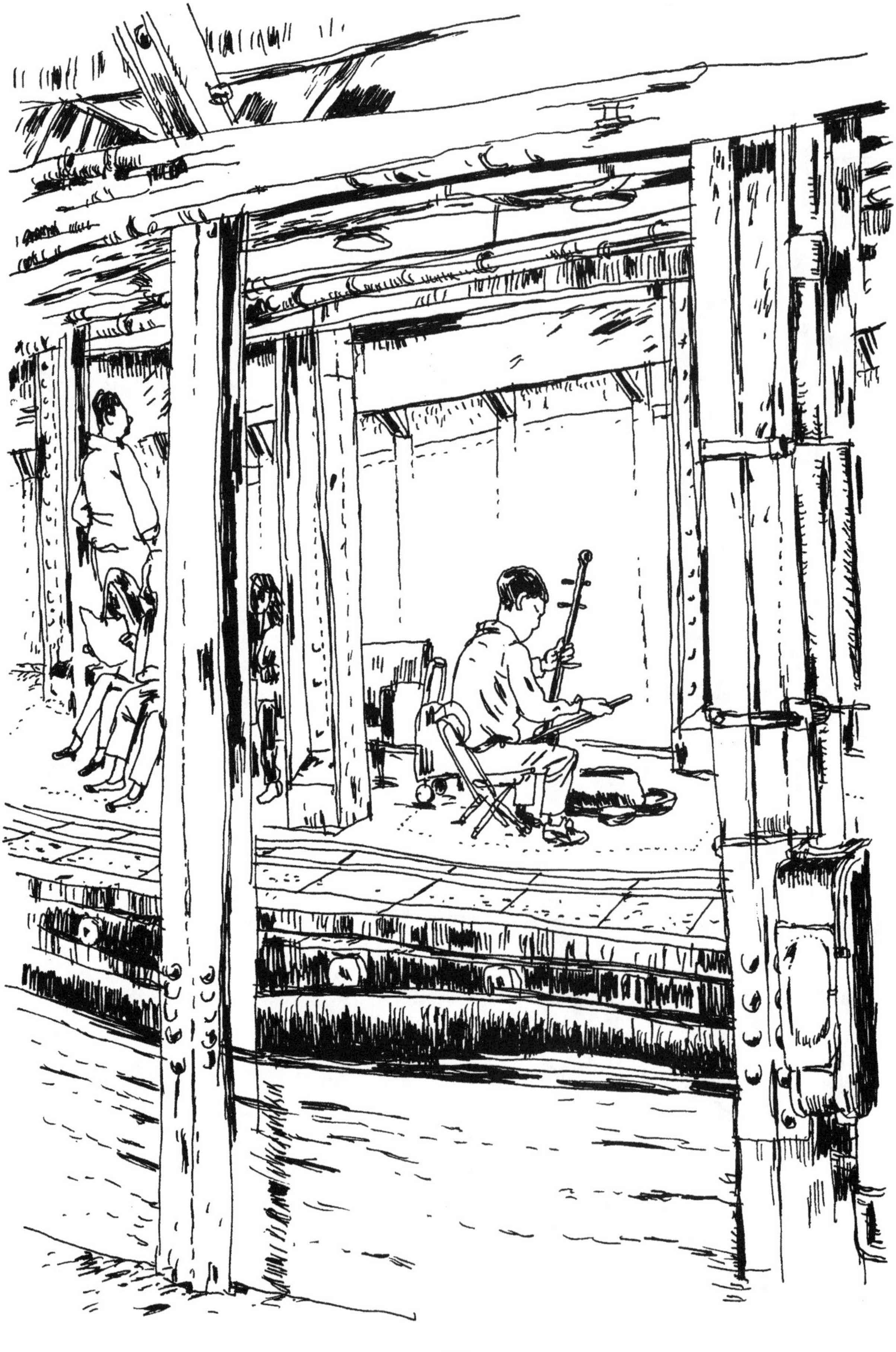

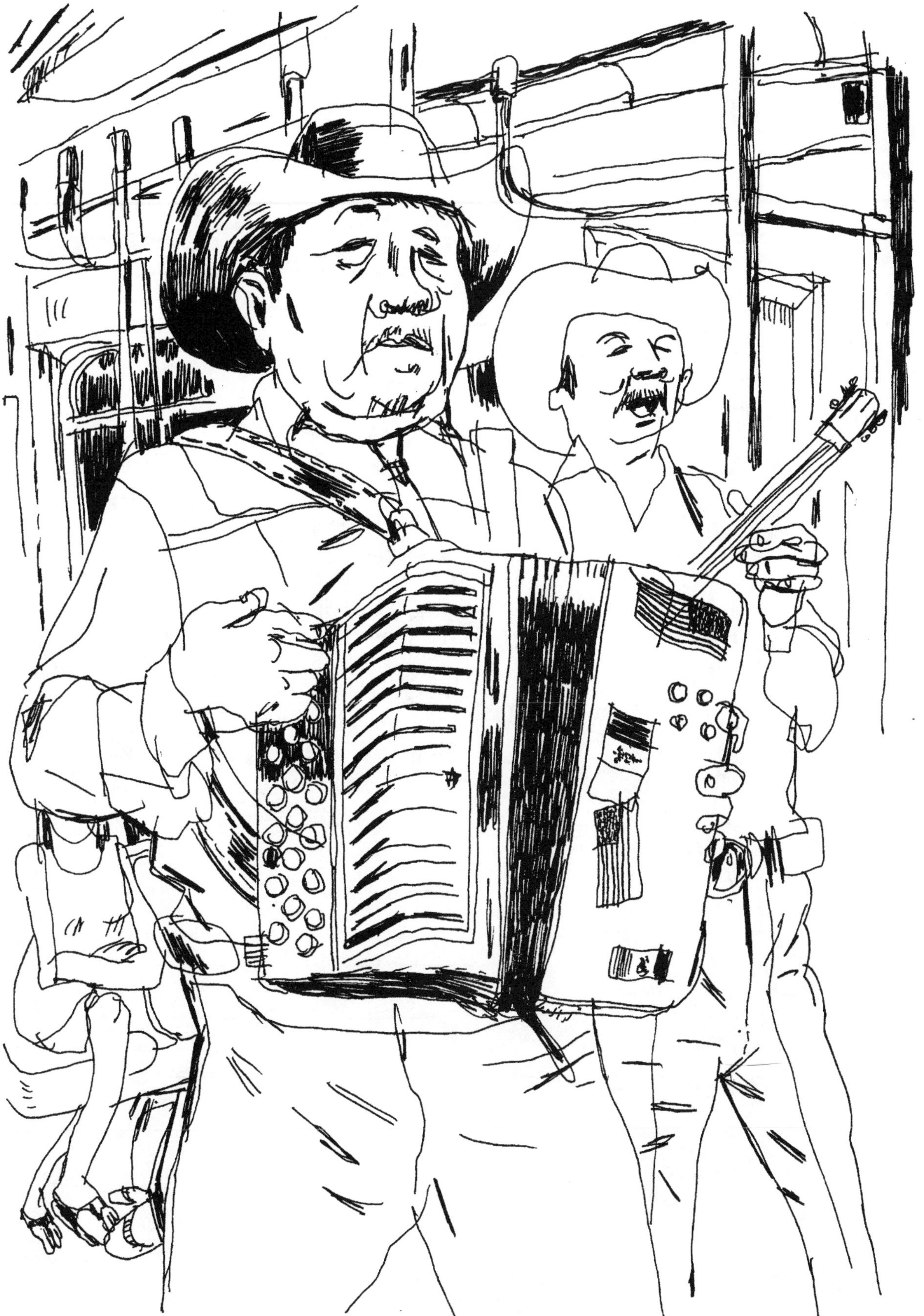

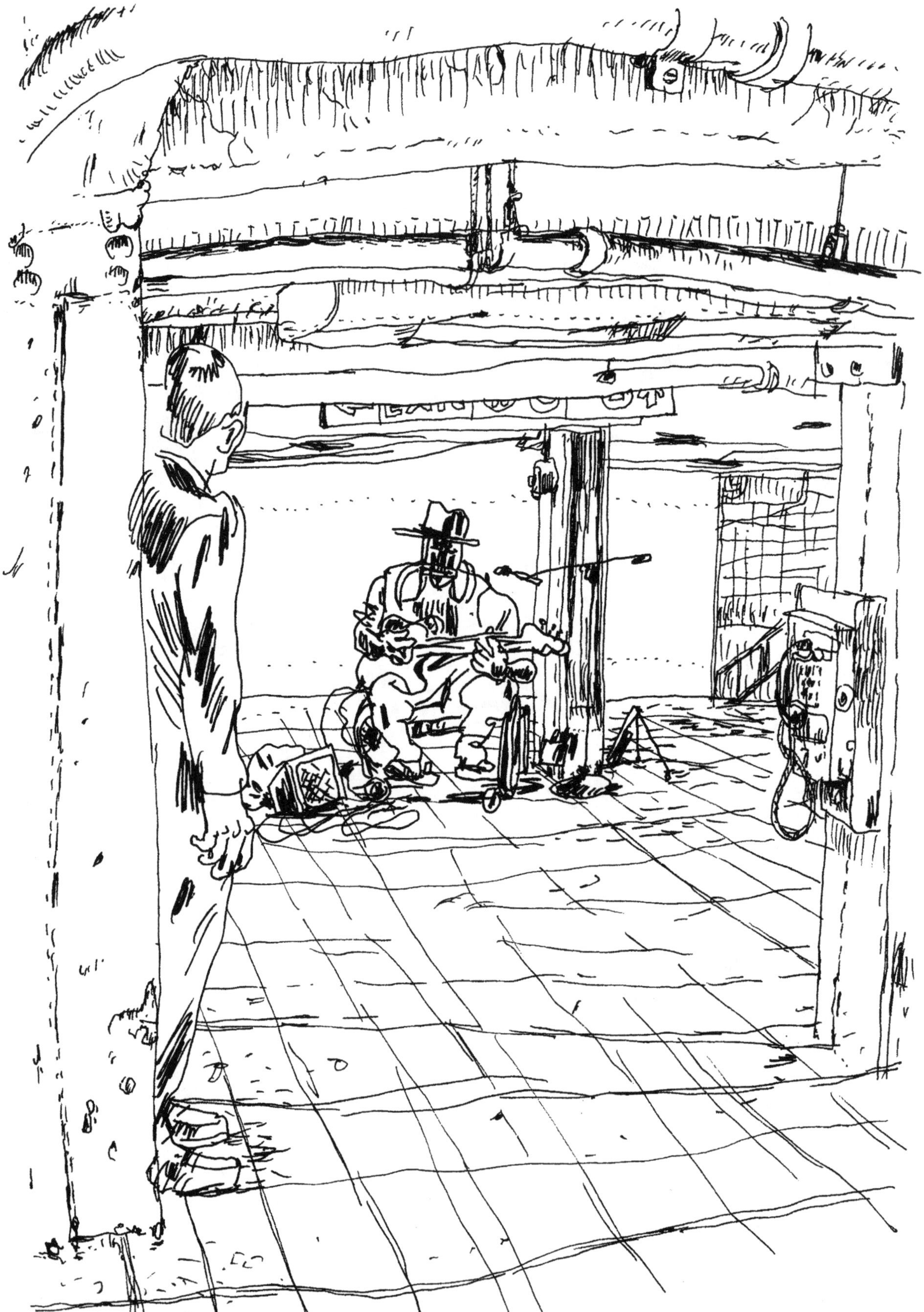

1920–GERMANY: KARLA ABRAHAMSEN REVEALS A DARK SECRET TO HER SON.

MY GOD!

IT'S TRUE, ERIK.

I'M SORRY. WE WAITED TO TELL YOU UNTIL WE FELT THE TIME WAS RIGHT.

WE KNOW IT HASN'T BEEN EASY BEING A STEP-SON... LET ALONE BEING...BEING...

BEING WHAT?! A BASTARD!!

After he was told the truth about his parentage and before becoming the world famous psychologist, he studied to become a painter.

NOW YOU TELL ME THAT NOT EVEN MY FATHER WAS MY FATHER!

Painting encouraged experimentation and close observation, activities that would later serve him well as a child psychologist.

WHO WAS MY FATHER, THEN?

IT'S NOT IMPORTANT.

HIS NAME WAS *ERIK*... LIKE *YOU*.

When he was 25 he became a patient of **Anna Freud** (Sigmund's daughter) and later, her colleague.

At the time **Freud's theories** about psychology and human development were **fresh** and **radical**.

...Erik...

AS YOU KNOW, SHORTLY AFTER YOU WERE BORN, *WALDEMAR SALOMONSEN*, YOUR *FIRST* STEPFATHER *LEFT ME*. HE *COULDN'T HANDLE* THE FACT THAT YOU WERE *NOT HIS SON*.

THREE YEARS LATER I FELL IN *LOVE* WITH YOUR *MOTHER*... *AND* WITH *YOU*, ERIK. AS FAR AS I AM CONCERNED, YOU ARE *MY SON*. MY SON, *ERIK HOMBURGER*.

I'M SURE THIS ALL COMES AS A *SHOCK* TO YOU, BUT YOU *MUST* KNOW THAT YOU'VE BEEN *LOVED*!

I *DO*... AND I'M *GRATEFUL* ...IT'S JUST...

As an '*Ego Psychologist*' he accepted **Freud's** notion about how **ego** and the **subconscious** determine **development**.

...I NEED SOME FRESH *AIR*.

To this he added his **own observations** about the **roles** of **society** and **environment** in shaping **identity**.

112

After years as a *child psychologist* he became renowned for his writing. Particularly *"Childhood & Society"* which contained the *"8 Stages."*

IT ALL MAKES SENSE...

...AND *NO* SENSE.

I'VE NEVER REALLY FIT IN.

THEY CALL ME *'THE ALBINO'* AT TEMPLE.

...AND *'JEW-BOY'* AT SCHOOL.

WHO *AM* I?

WHO IS *ANY*ONE?

He set forth a radical theory of *developmental psychology* that continues to have *impact.*

MY *FATHER'S* NAME WAS ERIK... *MY* NAME IS ERIK.

BUT I AM *NOT* ERIK *SALOMONSEN* OR ERIK *HOMBURGER.*

I AM *ERIK,* ERIK'S *SON.*

I AM ERIK ERIKSON.

SO, YOU SEE, QUESTIONS ABOUT IDENTITY WERE PERCOLATING IN HIS MIND YEARS BEFORE HE RAISED THE QUESTION OF...

HOW DO WE DEVELOP INTO HEALTHY MEMBERS OF SOCIETY??

HERE'S ONE MAN'S OPINION

Erik Erikson's

EIGHT STAGES OF

IDENTITY

DEVELOPMENT

At a clock factory parts are added one by one. After each part is added the clock should run fine. *BUT* if a wrong part is installed incorrectly...

WIND WIND WIND

tic - tock - tic - tock

SPROING!

For Erikson, the human being moves down life's assembly line *RESOLVING* specific *CONFLICTS* one by one.

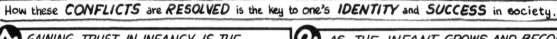

How these **CONFLICTS** are **RESOLVED** is the key to one's **IDENTITY** and **SUCCESS** in society.

---

1 GAINING TRUST IN INFANCY IS THE FOUNDATION FOR A HEALTHY IDENTITY:
TRUST   vs.   MISTRUST

GEE! WHAT SERVICE! I GET FED WHENEVER I CRY... EVEN AT 3 A.M.!

I NEVER GET WHAT I WANT WHEN I NEED IT!

WHY BOTHER CRYING?

---

2 AS THE INFANT GROWS AND BECOMES MOBILE, THIS IS THE NEXT CONFLICT:
AUTONOMY   vs.   SHAME & DOUBT

YAY! I CAN GO ANYWHERE AND DO *ANYTHING!!*

I CAN'T DO *ANYTHING* RIGHT AND *EVERYBODY* KNOWS IT / >sigh<

---

3 THE YOUNG CHILD MUST NEXT RESOLVE:
INITIATIVE   vs.   GUILT

HOW *CUTE!* HE WANTS TO SEE WHAT MAKES IT *TICK!*

YOU *WRETCH!* MY EXPENSIVE, PRICELESS, AND COSTLY CLOCK... *RUINED!!*

FUTURE INVENTOR

FUTURE DRIFTER

---

4 ELEMENTARY-AGED CHILDREN, PROPERLY ENCOURAGED, ARE RAVENOUS LEARNERS.
INDUSTRY   vs.   INFERIORITY

"SCALE MODEL OF THE *PARTHENON*" MADE OF TOOTH-PICKS & GLUE BY TIMMY.

"A HOUSE" MADE OF TOOTH-PICKS & GLUE BY CLYDE.

1ST PRIZE

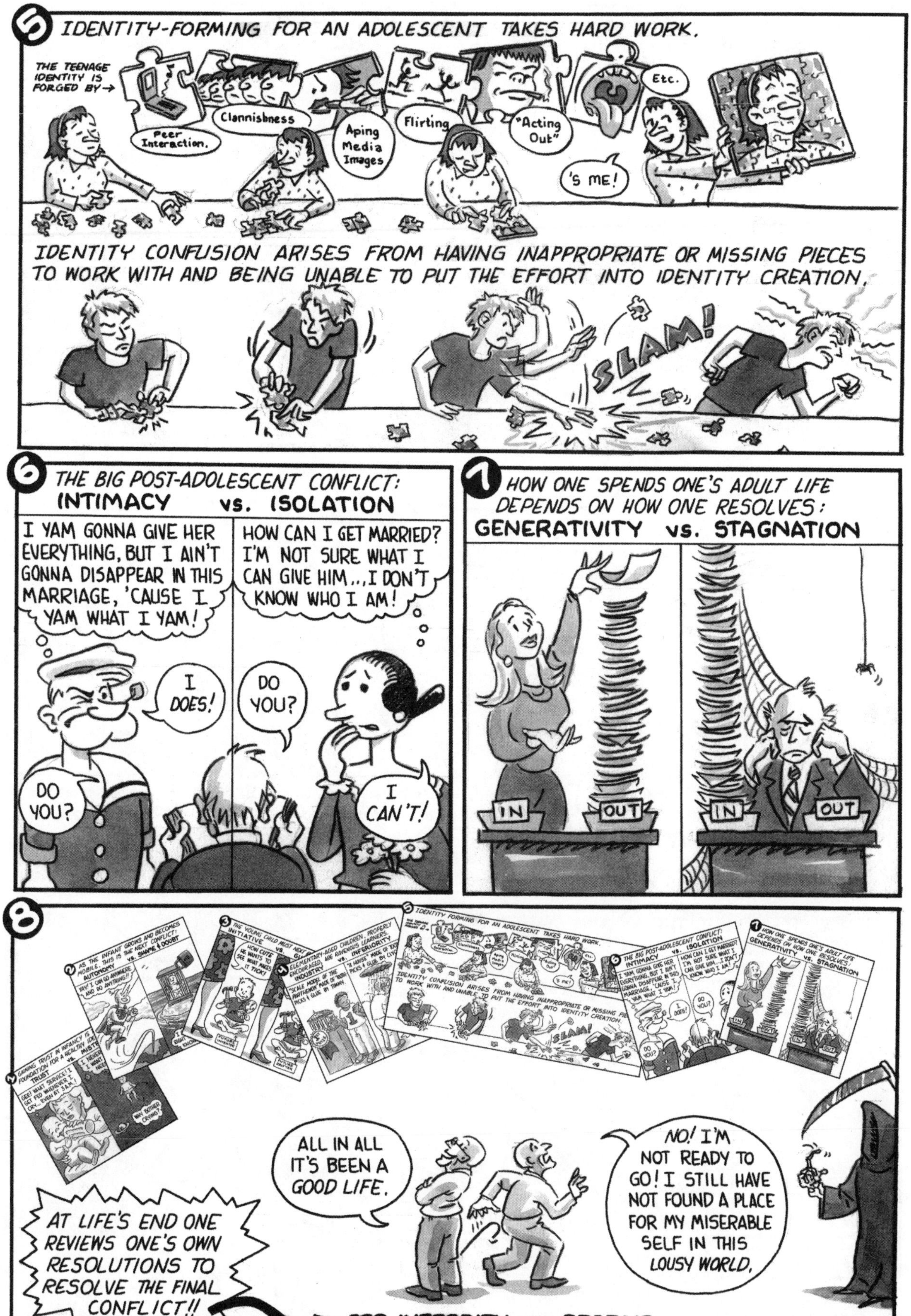
5
IDENTITY-FORMING FOR AN ADOLESCENT TAKES HARD WORK.
THE TEENAGE IDENTITY IS FORGED BY →
Peer Interaction.
Clannishness
Aping Media Images
Flirting
"Acting Out"
Etc.
'S ME!
IDENTITY CONFUSION ARISES FROM HAVING INAPPROPRIATE OR MISSING PIECES TO WORK WITH AND BEING UNABLE TO PUT THE EFFORT INTO IDENTITY CREATION.
SLAM!
6
THE BIG POST-ADOLESCENT CONFLICT:
INTIMACY vs. ISOLATION
I YAM GONNA GIVE HER EVERYTHING, BUT I AIN'T GONNA DISAPPEAR IN THIS MARRIAGE, 'CAUSE I YAM WHAT I YAM!
I DOES!
DO YOU?
HOW CAN I GET MARRIED? I'M NOT SURE WHAT I CAN GIVE HIM...I DON'T KNOW WHO I AM!
DO YOU?
I CAN'T!
7
HOW ONE SPENDS ONE'S ADULT LIFE DEPENDS ON HOW ONE RESOLVES:
GENERATIVITY vs. STAGNATION
IN
OUT
IN
OUT
8
ALL IN ALL IT'S BEEN A GOOD LIFE.
NO! I'M NOT READY TO GO! I STILL HAVE NOT FOUND A PLACE FOR MY MISERABLE SELF IN THIS LOUSY WORLD.
AT LIFE'S END ONE REVIEWS ONE'S OWN RESOLUTIONS TO RESOLVE THE FINAL CONFLICT!!
EGO INTEGRITY vs. DESPAIR

1948-CALIFORNIA: ERIKSON AND HIS WIFE REVEAL A DARK SECRET TO THEIR CHILDREN.

MY GOD!

IT'S TRUE, KIDS.

WE THOUGHT WE SHOULD **WAIT** UNTIL YOU WERE **OLDER** BEFORE WE **TOLD** YOU ABOUT YOUR **BROTHER.**

OUR...BROTHER?

WHO WE THOUGHT **DIED AT BIRTH!!**

IT WAS **DIFFICULT...** THE WHOLE... **EXPERIENCE.**

Erikson began work on the **Stages** in earnest after the birth of his **disabled son**, Neil, in 1944. **'Childhood & Society'** was published in 1950 but didn't become a **hit** 'til the 60s as an affordable paperback for college Psychology Majors.

WHEN WE FOUND OUT THE CHILD'S... **NEIL'S...** CONDITION WE DIDN'T KNOW WHAT TO DO.

EVERYONE ADVISED US THAT THE **ONLY OPTION** FOR NEIL WAS THE **INSTITUTION.**

Issues of personal identity within society were of central **importance** to the 60s generation who **embraced** and largely **lionized** Erikson.

NEIL... NEIL... NEIL ERIKSON.

AN **INSTITUTION** FOR BABIES WITH **DOWN SYNDROME?!**

YES, AND FOR OTHER ...*ABNORMALITIES.*

AND *THAT'S* WHERE HE'S BEEN ALL THESE YEARS?

Often overlooked is Erikson's *method* of inquiry. He based his theories on studying the psychology of *real* people and how they *interacted* within a specific *social context*. *This* was a kind of *innovation.*

HOW COULD YOU *DO* THAT?

HOW COULD YOU *NOT TELL* US?

WE'RE...SORRY...

BUT WE DID WHAT WE DID AND, WELL, THAT'S THAT.

Erikson was interested in how the *'Normal'* child becomes the *'Normal'* man through *resolving* life's *conflicts.*

C'MON, JOAN. I NEED SOME FRESH AIR.

Together with his collaborator (his wife, Joan), they began their *research* in their *'Normal'* home with their *'Normal'* children.

In *reaction* to unsettling questions about his *own identity* as a child, Erikson was *propelled* on his lifelong course of study.

WELL, *THAT* WAS AWFUL. THEY MUST THINK US *BEASTS*, ERIK.

THAT WOULD BE NORMAL.

NORMAL... YES...NORMAL.

THEY'LL GET OVER IT.

OUR KIDS ARE AT THE RIGHT STAGE TO ACCEPT THE *TRUTH.*

THERE YOU GO WITH YOUR *'STAGES'* AGAIN.

OUR KIDS ARE NORMAL AND *NORMALITY* PROCEEDS *STAGE BY STAGE.*

In *reaction* to the *birth* of his Down Syndrome son, Neil, Erikson began creating his *dynamic schema* of the *development* of the *normal child.*

STAGE..."ALL THE WORLD'S A STAGE."

"... AND THE MEN AND WOMEN MERELY PLAYERS."

End

PAUL KAPASIK 2008

DVORAK

by Alec Longstreth

IN 1962, SEATTLE HOSTED THE WORLD'S FAIR. NEARLY **TEN MILLION** PEOPLE CAME TO SEE THE "CENTURY 21 EXPOSITION," WHICH FEATURED ALL OF THE LATEST SPACE RACE TECHNOLOGY AND VISIONS OF A MORE EFFICIENT FUTURE.

THE MONORAIL!

ONE SUCH VISITOR WAS A WRITER FROM MISSISSAUGA, ONTARIO, NAMED **ROBERT PARKINSON.**

WHILE IN TOWN FOR THE FAIR, PARKINSON DECIDED TO LOOK UP A RETIRED PROFESSOR OF EDUCATIONAL PSYCHOLOGY FROM THE UNIVERSITY OF WASHINGTON...

DR. AUGUST DVORAK, INVENTOR OF THE DVORAK SIMPLIFIED KEYBOARD LAYOUT!

≡SIGH≡ ALL RIGHT, COME IN IF YOU MUST.

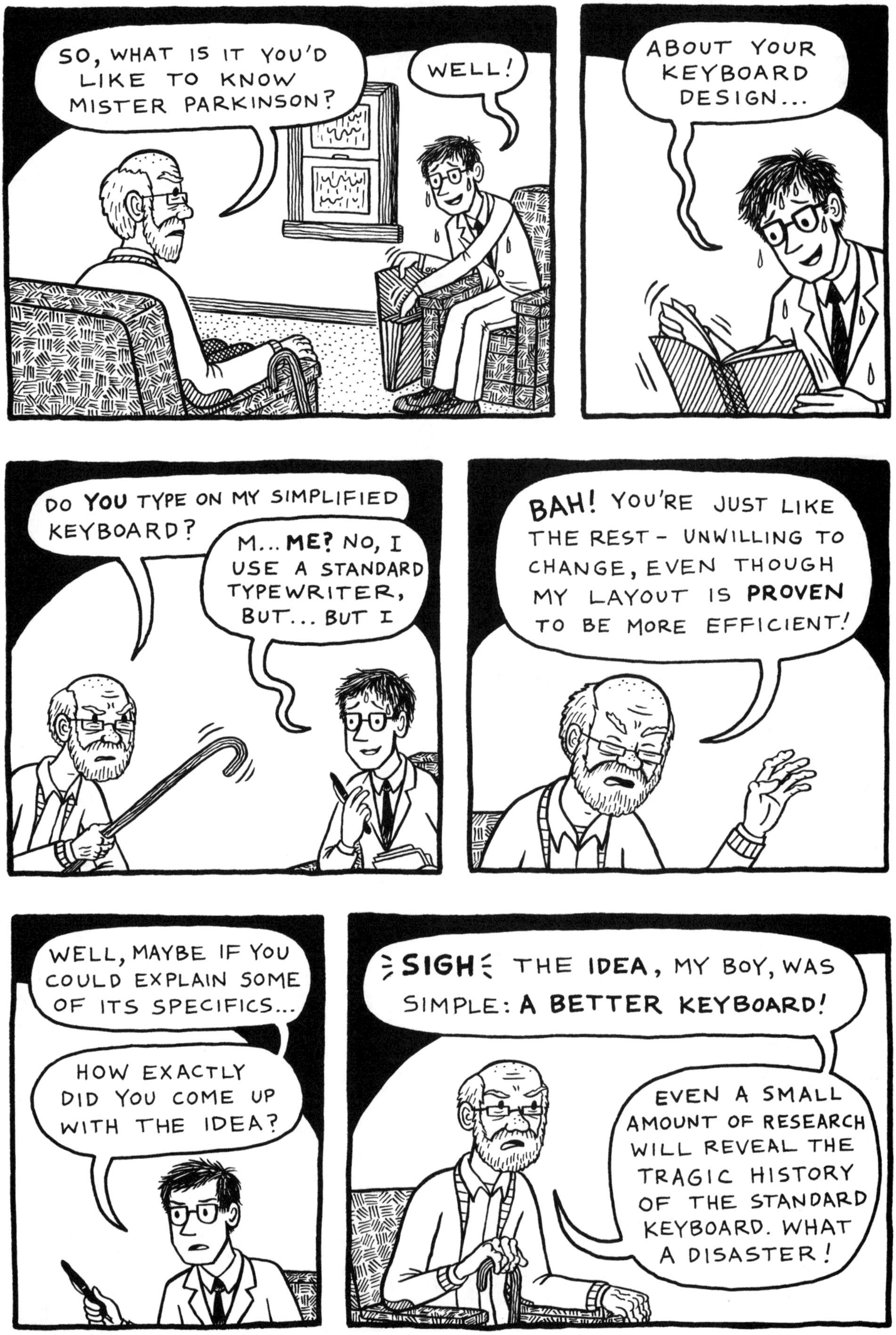
SO, WHAT IS IT YOU'D LIKE TO KNOW MISTER PARKINSON?
WELL!
ABOUT YOUR KEYBOARD DESIGN...
DO **YOU** TYPE ON MY SIMPLIFIED KEYBOARD?
M... **ME?** NO, I USE A STANDARD TYPEWRITER, BUT... BUT I
BAH! YOU'RE JUST LIKE THE REST - UNWILLING TO CHANGE, EVEN THOUGH MY LAYOUT IS **PROVEN** TO BE MORE EFFICIENT!
WELL, MAYBE IF YOU COULD EXPLAIN SOME OF ITS SPECIFICS...
HOW EXACTLY DID YOU COME UP WITH THE IDEA?
SIGH THE **IDEA**, MY BOY, WAS SIMPLE: **A BETTER KEYBOARD!**
EVEN A SMALL AMOUNT OF RESEARCH WILL REVEAL THE TRAGIC HISTORY OF THE STANDARD KEYBOARD. WHAT A DISASTER!

CHRIS SHOLES WAS A GOOD INVENTOR, BUT WHEN HIS TYPEWRITER PROTOTYPE JAMMED, HE MADE A HORRIBLE MISTAKE.

HMMM... I'LL HAVE TO FIX THE TYPE-BAR MECHANISMS.

OR **WAIT!** INSTEAD, I COULD JUST REARRANGE THE KEYBOARD!

HE RANDOMLY PLACED COMMON LETTER PAIRS FAR APART TO PREVENT JAMMING AND UNFORTUNATELY, IT **WORKED.** THE TYPEWRITER WAS RELEASED TO THE PUBLIC IN 1873.

THAT OUGHT TO BE GOOD ENOUGH FOR NOW...

BY 1878, SHOLES HAD SOLD HIS INVENTION TO **REMINGTON,** WHICH TOOK OVER PRODUCTION AND IMPROVED UPON HIS DESIGN. THEY WERE SOON SELLING 100,000 TYPEWRITERS A YEAR!

PEOPLE ALL ACROSS THE COUNTRY BEGAN MEMORIZING THIS RANDOM ARRANGEMENT OF KEYS. IN 1888 FRANK McGURRIN DEVELOPED A METHOD FOR PEOPLE TO "TOUCH TYPE" WITH ALL TEN FINGERS.

Q-W-E-R-T-Y

KLAK KLAK KLAK KLAK KLAK KLAK KLA

BUT BY THEN, THE TYPE-BAR MECHANISMS HAD BEEN FIXED, SO IN 1889 SHOLES SUBMITTED A PATENT FOR A NEW, **IMPROVED** KEYBOARD.

AHHH, THIS LAYOUT MAKES SO MUCH MORE **SENSE!**

FIVE MONTHS LATER, SHOLES WAS **DEAD.** HIS PATENT **WAS** APPROVED... BUT IT TOOK **SEVEN YEARS,** AND BY THEN IT DIDN'T STAND A CHANCE... "QWERTY" HAD BECOME UBIQUITOUS.

NOT TO MENTION THE **THIRTY-SIX** ADDITIONAL YEARS BETWEEN HIS PATENT AND YOURS.

≥SIGH≤

DID YOU BASE YOUR KEYBOARD ON SHOLES'S REDESIGN? I NOTICED THE HOME ROWS SHARE SOME OF THE SAME LETTERS...

ON **SHOLES?!** HA! SHOLES WAS AN **INVENTOR.** **I** AM A **SCIENTIST.** DO YOU HAVE ANY IDEA HOW MUCH RESEARCH WENT INTO MY DESIGN?

I RESEARCHED LETTER FREQUENCIES AND COMMON LETTER PAIRS, OR "DIGRAPHS." I STUDIED THE PHYSIOLOGY OF THE HUMAN HAND: RELATIVE FINGER STRENGTHS, FINGER MOBILITY AND COORDINATION!

ALL OF THIS DATA HAD TO BE COMBINED, CORRELATED, ANALYZED AND OPTIMIZED!

HOW ON EARTH DID YOU APPROACH SUCH A COMPLEX PROBLEM?

WELL, I FIGURED SINCE I WAS TRYING TO **OPTIMIZE** THE KEYBOARD, I'D START BY CONSULTING THE RENOWNED EFFICIENCY EXPERT **DR. FRANK GILBRETH!**

FROM **CHEAPER BY THE DOZEN?**

YES, THE "FATHER OF TIME" HIMSELF!

UNDER HIS DIRECTION, I BEGAN THE RESEARCH THAT LED TO MY KEYBOARD DESIGN.

I RECEIVED FUNDING FROM THE CARNEGIE FOUNDATION, WHICH I USED TO CAPTURE MOTION PICTURE FOOTAGE OF PEOPLE **USING** A TYPEWRITER. THIS ALLOWED ME TO STUDY THE MOVEMENT OF HANDS AND FINGERS TYPING IN SLOW MOTION.

USING THIS DATA, AND ALL OF MY OTHER RESEARCH, I BEGAN CREATING **HUNDREDS** OF LAYOUTS. I STUDIED EACH ONE, REFINING THE KEY PLACEMENT, IMPROVING THE DESIGN.

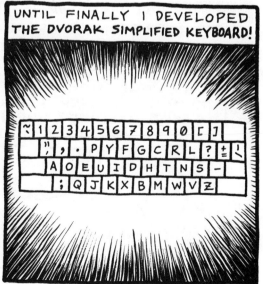

UNTIL FINALLY I DEVELOPED **THE DVORAK SIMPLIFIED KEYBOARD!**

I PLACED ALL OF THE VOWELS AND THE MOST COMMON CONSONANTS ON THE EASY-TO-REACH HOME ROW. THIS BROUGHT **70%** OF ALL KEYSTROKES TO THE HOME ROW, COMPARED TO ONLY **31%** USING QWERTY.

QWERTY ⬆
A S D F G H J K L ;

SEMICOLON?!

ONLY **ONE** VOWEL!

DVORAK ⬆
A O E U I D H T N S

THE PLACEMENT OF THE REMAINING KEYS ALSO IMPROVED TYPING SPEED AND COMFORT, WHILE REDUCING ERRORS.

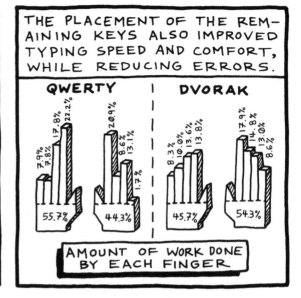

QWERTY | DVORAK

AMOUNT OF WORK DONE BY EACH FINGER

ON MAY 21ST, 1932, I FILED A PATENT FOR MY KEYBOARD LAYOUT. IT WAS APPROVED FOUR YEARS LATER, ON MAY 12TH, 1936.

I IMMEDIATELY CONTACTED A NUMBER OF TYPEWRITER MANUFACTURERS TO TRY AND CONVINCE THEM TO SELL A DVORAK TYPEWRITER.

LET ME SEE IF I UNDERSTAND CORRECTLY...

BUT THIS WAS ALL HAPPENING DURING **THE GREAT DEPRESSION** AND MOST COMPANIES WERE COMPLETELY BROKE!

THIS WOULD ALLOW **ONE** TYPIST TO DO **TWICE** AS MUCH WORK WITH THE **SAME** MACHINE? WHY, WE'D SELL FEWER TYPEWRITERS!

BUT I WAS NOT GOING TO GIVE UP **THAT** EASILY!

TO INCREASE AWARENESS, I SET UP A STUDY TO TEACH MY LAYOUT TO OVER 2,700 HIGH SCHOOL SENIORS IN A TACOMA, WASHINGTON SCHOOL DISTRICT.

A-O-E-U-I

KLAK
K
KLAK
KLAK KL.

THE STUDY PROVED THAT THE STUDENTS COULD LEARN THE DVORAK LAYOUT IN **ONE-THIRD** THE TIME IT TOOK TO LEARN QWERTY. BUT A SCHOOL BOARD OFFICIAL LOOKING TO BE RE-ELECTED HAD MY STUDY **CANCELED** FOR HIS OWN POLITICAL LEVERAGE.

I HAVE SURVEYED OUR LOCAL BUSINESSES AND NOT **ONE** OF THEM EMPLOYS A "DVORAK" TYPEWRITER!

P.T.A.

HAVING FAILED ON A LOCAL LEVEL, I INSTEAD TRIED TO GAIN **WORLD-WIDE** RECOGNITION FOR MY LAYOUT, BY COMPETING IN THE **INTERNATIONAL COMMERCIAL SCHOOLS CONTEST** FOR TYPING.

NEXT, FROM SEATTLE...

MY STUDENTS SWEPT THE FIELD! OVER A SEVEN-YEAR PERIOD, THEY PLACED FIRST IN THEIR CATEGORIES **TEN TIMES.** BUT IT WAS NOT ALWAYS EASY...

I.C.S.C.

IN 1937, THE I.C.S.C. COMMITTEE TRIED TO DISQUALIFY MY STUDENTS, STATING THAT THEY WERE "UNFAIR COMPETITION."

BUT IT COST US $1,600 TO TRAVEL HERE TO CHICAGO!

I THREATENED TO TELL THE NEWSPAPERS THAT THE I.C.S.C. WAS TRYING TO **HOLD BACK** THE SKILL OF TYPING, INSTEAD OF **ADVANCING** IT. THEY GRUDGINGLY ALLOWED MY STUDENTS TO COMPETE.

THE NEXT YEAR OUR SPECIAL DVORAK TYPEWRITERS WERE **SABOTAGED.** SOMEONE RESET THE MARGIN STOPS JUST ENOUGH TO CAUSE LINE LENGTH AND PARAGRAPHING ERRORS.

DISQUALIFIED.

AFTER THAT, I HAD TO HIRE SECURITY GUARDS TO WATCH OUR TYPEWRITERS WHILE WE WERE OUT OF OUR HOTEL ROOM.

DID YOUR LAYOUT GAIN SOME RECOGNITION? SURELY THE I.C.S.C. COULDN'T IGNORE HOW EFFECTIVELY YOUR KEYBOARD PERFORMED!

≷SIGH≷ I'M AFRAID NOT, MY BOY... THE CONTESTS WERE CALLED OFF A FEW YEARS LATER, WHEN **WORLD WAR TWO** BROKE OUT.

OF COURSE. DID **YOU** SERVE IN THE WAR?

CERTAINLY! **EVERY** ABLE-BODIED MAN JOINED THE MILITARY!

EVEN MY KEYBOARD LAYOUT JOINED IN THE WAR EFFORT. OR AT LEAST IT **TRIED** TO...

IN 1944, A GROUP OF MANAGEMENT ENGINEERS IN THE U.S. NAVY CONDUCTED AN EXPERIMENT, RETRAINING STANDARD TYPISTS ON MY SIMPLIFIED KEYBOARD LAYOUT.

D-H-T-N-S

KLAK KLAK KLAK KLAK

THE DVORAK TYPISTS INCREASED THEIR PRODUCTIVITY BY AN AVERAGE OF **74%**!

DVORAK

THE NAVY PUT IN A REQUEST FOR 2,000 DVORAK TYPEWRITERS.

THINK OF THE INCREASED EFFICIENCY, SIR!

BUT ALL OF THE TYPEWRITER MANUFACTURERS WERE BUSY MAKING **WAR GOODS**, SO STANDARD TYPEWRITERS WOULD HAVE TO BE **CONVERTED** TO DVORAK AT A COST OF $25 PER UNIT!

$50,000?! THERE'S A **WAR** ON YOU KNOW!

AFTER THE WAR, I SAW THE NEED FOR **ANOTHER** NEW KEYBOARD LAYOUT, TO AID ALL OF THE VETERANS RETURNING HOME WITH MISSING LIMBS.

I DEVELOPED ONE-HANDED KEYBOARD LAYOUTS BASED ON MY PREVIOUS RESEARCH. THEY HAVE BEEN HELPING AMPUTEES TYPE EVER SINCE!

KLAK

KLAK

'LEFT-HANDED' DVORAK

127

SO THAT'S MY STORY, LAD. I'VE SPENT THE LAST THIRTY YEARS OF MY LIFE TRYING TO INTRODUCE MY KEYBOARD LAYOUT, AND I'VE BEEN **BLOCKED** AT EVERY TURN!

BUT WHY DO YOU THINK THAT **IS**, DR. DVORAK?

THE SAME REASON IT TOOK 35 TO 70 YEARS FOR THE RAILROADS, RADIO, TELEPHONES, AIRPLANES AND YES, EVEN THE **AUTOMOBILE** TO GAIN GENERAL ACCEPTANCE.

EACH REQUIRED INVESTMENT OF TIME, MONEY AND EFFORT TO IMPLEMENT. AND EACH WAS OPPOSED BY THOSE WHO HAD INVESTMENTS IN THE STATUS QUO!

BUT SURELY WE ARE MORE PROGRESSIVE TODAY! DON'T YOU THINK THE—

BAH... I'M TIRED OF TRYING TO DO SOMETHING WORTHWHILE FOR THE HUMAN RACE. THEY SIMPLY DON'T WANT TO CHANGE!

ROBERT PARKINSON COMPILED HIS FINDINGS IN AN ARTICLE ENTITLED "THE DVORAK SIMPLIFIED KEYBOARD: FORTY YEARS OF FRUSTRATION." IT WAS PUBLISHED IN **COMPUTERS AND AUTOMATION MAGAZINE** IN 1972.

THREE YEARS LATER, DR. AUGUST DVORAK DIED, ON OCTOBER 10TH, 1975.

EVER SINCE THAT DAY, DR. DVORAK'S STUDENTS, AND MANY OTHERS WHO SAW THE LOGIC OF HIS KEYBOARD, HAVE BEEN CARRYING ON HIS FIGHT.

AFTER YEARS OF STRUGGLE, A DVORAK ENTHUSIAST AT THE **AMERICAN NATIONAL STANDARDS INSTITUTE** FINALLY GOT DVORAK APPROVED AS AN **OFFICIAL** TYPING ALTERNATIVE IN 1982.

DVORAK SIMPLIFIED KEYBOARD LAYOUT

APPROVED ANSI 1982

AT THE TIME, MORE PEOPLE MADE THEIR LIVING WITH A TYPEWRITER THAN WITH ANY OTHER BUSINESS MACHINE IN THE WORLD. AND THAT WAS **BEFORE** THE ADVENT OF THE DESKTOP COMPUTER!

ELECTRONIC TYPEWRITER

CLK CLK CLK CLK CLK

SOME OF THE EARLIEST **APPLE COMPUTER** MODELS CAME WITH DVORAK, INCLUDING THE **APPLE IIc**, RELEASED IN 1984.

KEYBOARD TOGGLES BETWEEN DVORAK AND QWERTY

A FEW YEARS LATER, LINDA LEWIS AND RANDY CASSINGHAM TRAVELED TO THE **MICROSOFT** HEADQUARTERS, WHERE THEY MANAGED TO CONVINCE THE COMPANY TO INCLUDE DVORAK IN ITS **WINDOWS** OPERATING SYSTEM.

THESE DAYS, DVORAK COMES PRE-INSTALLED ON **EVERY** TYPE OF COMPUTER, NO MATTER WHICH OPERATING SYSTEM ONE USES.

IT IS A SIMPLE MATTER OF CHANGING A FEW SETTINGS. IT HAS NEVER BEEN EASIER TO TRY THE DVORAK SIMPLIFIED KEYBOARD LAYOUT!

CLICK
CLICK

AND WITH THE WIDESPREAD USE OF COMPUTERS IN THE WORKPLACE AND AT HOME, TYPING HAS NEVER BEEN MORE IMPORTANT THAN TODAY!

TK TK TK TK TK TK TK TK TK TK TK TK TK TK

EMAIL

THE REDUCTION IN FINGER MOVEMENT ALSO MEANS THAT DVORAK CAN BE HELPFUL FOR TYPISTS SUFFERING FROM **REPETITIVE STRESS INJURIES.**

AHHH, TYPING DVORAK IS **SO** MUCH MORE COMFORTABLE!

TK TK TK TK

THE INTERNET HAS MADE IT EASIER THAN EVER TO SPREAD THE WORD ABOUT DVORAK. EVERY DAY NEW PEOPLE ARE MAKING THE SWITCH AND BENEFITTING FROM DR. DVORAK'S INVENTION!

DVzine.org

ALEC

Coney Island Rumination

WORDS AND PICTURES BY PAUL HOPPE

IT USED TO BE THE PLACE WHERE THE WORLD CAME TO PLAY. FANTASTICAL ATTRACTIONS, UNLIKE ANY PLACE IN THE ENTIRE WORLD.

TODAY, ITS RICKETY, COLORFUL RIDES HAVE A NOSTALGIC APPEAL.

SHADOWS OF A BETTER PAST ARE BLEACHED BY THE SUN.

A PLACE WHERE NEW YORK TAKES A BREAK.

IT'S A PLACE WITH A LOT OF SOUL (AND OCCASIONALLY SALSA)...

...OF SIMPLE PLEASURES GARNISHED WITH RUSTY MELANCHOLY.

IT'S RICH WITH MANY STORIES.

SONNY THE GUARD DOG

...OR JUST FOR A BRIEF ESCAPE FROM THE DAILY GRIND.

MANY, MANY PHOTOGRAPHS OF OLD CONEY ISLAND ON THE WALLS

RUBY'S
Coney Island
NY
BUD LIGHT

WILLIE

THERE ARE PEOPLE LOOKING FOR A BETTER LIFE...

TICKETS

ENTER

ARAY'S BACKPACK

ARAY FROM KAZAKHSTAN

133

AND THERE'S THE OCEAN, OF COURSE.

IT PROVIDES US WITH A COOL BREEZE, A SENSE OF PEACE, AND... FISH.

STEEPLECHASE PIER

SUNBATHERS FROM ALL WALKS OF LIFE...

YA KNOW, I WAS YOUNG AND IN LOVE...

...SIT NEXT TO EACH OTHER...

... LOOKING FOR A BREATH OF FRESH AIR.

THE PAST IS ALWAYS PRESENT BEHIND THE
PEELING PAINTS AND DIRTY FACADES.

FORMER "CHILD'S" RESTAURANT LATER USED BY A CANDY MANU-FACTURER AND A BOOK DISTRIBUTOR

BUILT IN 1924

LIVING LANDMARKS TELL STORIES
ABOUT MORE GLORIOUS TIMES.

OTHERS HAVE BEEN SILENT
FOR A LONG TIME.

PRIME MEATS

FOR YOUR BARBEUE SPECIALS

JIMMY PRINCE AT MAJOR'S MEAT MARKET SINCE 1949

PARACHUTE JUMP

FROM 1939 WORLD'S FAIR

THE ARTIFACTS ARE EVERYWHERE,
YOU JUST HAVE TO KEEP YOUR
EYES OPEN.

BUT ALL OF THEM ALSO REPRESENT
HOPE AND POTENTIAL FOR THE FUTURE.

UTILITY POLE FROM OLD TROLLEY SERVICE, OVER 100 YEARS OLD.

HOTEL SURF ROOMS

THE UNIQUE ATMOSPHERE HAS ATTRACTED A NEW GENERATION OF ARTISTS, ACTIVISTS AND ODDBALLS.

MERMAID PARADE ©

MERGING THE OLD WITH THE NEW AND ADDING THE HIP...

DONNY VOMIT FROM THE SIDESHOWS BY THE SEASHORE

...A NEW CONEY CULTURE HAS BEEN EMERGING.

BLACK SCORPION FROM TEXAS

HEATHER HOLLIDAY, ALSO CONTORTIONIST, AND FIRE-EATER

FILM, FASHION AND ALL THE BIG ENTERTAINMENT STAPLES LIKE TO DIP THEIR FEET HERE ON OCCASION.

AS WELL AS OTHER KINDS OF ARTISTS.

BUT THE CHARM OF THE CRUMMY CAN'T QUITE COVER UP THE PROBLEMS.

THERE IS A STANDOFF BETWEEN THE CITY AND PRIVATE INVESTORS...

EMPTY LOTS

...ABOUT REDEVELOPMENT AND PRESERVATION, AND QUALITY OF LIFE.

THEY ALL WANT TO "FIX" CONEY ISLAND IN THEIR OWN WAYS.

THE BULLDOZERS STAND READY TO FINISH THE JOB.

THE FUTURE OF CONEY ISLAND

CONEY ISLAND USED TO BE A PLACE UNLIKE ANY OTHER IN THE WORLD.
TODAY, WITH ITS RUST, DUST, AND FADED MEMORIES, IT STILL IS.
AND TOMORROW? WE'LL HAVE TO SEE... THERE'S ALWAYS ANOTHER SUMMER.

WITH MANY THANKS
TO CONEY ISLAND USA,
THE SIDESHOW, THE MUSEUM,
THE RESIDENTS AND THE ONES WHO KEEP IT ALL RUNNING,
JIMMY PRINCE AND EVERYBODY WHO TOLD ME THEIR STORY.

AN ENCOUNTER WITH
RICHARD PETERSON

BY
BRENDAN B.

SOMETIMES WHEN THE BOREDOM OF EVERYDAY **LIFE** BECOMES TOO MUCH TO BEAR, I'LL WALK THE STREETS AND NEIGHBORHOODS OF **NEW YORK CITY** IN SEARCH OF A STORY THAT MIGHT HELP CHANGE MY **PERSPECTIVE**.

IT SEEMS TO ME THAT THE BEST REMINDER THAT **LIFE** ISN'T SO **ORDINARY** IS TO TAKE A CLOSER LOOK AT THE TYPICAL **GOINGS ON** OF THE CITY AROUND YOU.

ON A RECENT OCCASION, I DECIDED TO VISIT THE **CHESS PLAYERS** AT THE SOUTHWEST CORNER OF **WASHINGTON SQUARE PARK** IN NEW YORK'S GREENWICH VILLAGE.

THIS CORNER OF THE PARK HAS BEEN HOST TO A LIVELY **CHESS** SCENE FOR **DECADES**.

IT'S SEEN MANY A CHESS "**GRAND MASTER**" PASS THROUGH, INCLUDING THE WORLD-FAMOUS **GENIUS** BOBBY FISCHER AND HIS **MENTORS** BEFORE HIM.

I HAD BEEN CONSIDERING PROFILING THE **CHESS** SCENE THERE FOR SOME TIME — MAYBE THERE WOULD BE A **STORY** TO FIND.

BUT THE CORNER AND ITS HISTORY HAS BEEN THOROUGHLY **DOCUMENTED** AND I WASN'T SURE I WOULD BE ABLE TO ADD ANYTHING **NEW** TO A PLACE THAT WAS SUCH WELL-TREAD GROUND FOR THE **REPORTERS** AND **STORYTELLERS** BEFORE ME.

STILL, I FELT PERHAPS I COULD FIND AN **ANGLE** — SOMETHING OR SOMEONE THAT MAY HAVE GONE OVERLOOKED OR IGNORED.

THE FIRST DAY I SHOWED UP AT THE CORNER, THE PLAYERS WEREN'T SHY ABOUT TRYING TO **DRAG** ME INTO A GAME.

C'MON MAN, YOU WANT A **GAME**?

WHADDYA SAY, **FIVE** BUCKS A GAME?

ALTHOUGH I MORE OR LESS KNOW THE **RULES** AND SOME **BASIC** STRATEGIES OF THE GAME, I AM BY **NO MEANS** A GOOD CHESS PLAYER— I KNEW I'D BE HUSTLED OUT OF A FEW BUCKS IF I CAVED IN AND SAT DOWN FOR A ROUND WITH **ANY ONE** OF THEM.

C'MON, WHADDYA **SAY**?

AFTER SOME TIME OF LOOKING OVER SHOULDERS AND WATCHING THE GUYS INTERACT WITH ONE ANOTHER, I GRAVITATED TOWARD ONE OF THE **FRIENDLIER**, LESS **AGGRESSIVE** FELLOWS THERE.

HE SEEMED **ABOVE** THE HUSTLING RACKET TO SOME DEGREE, BUT IT DOESN'T MEAN HE WASN'T INTERESTED IN MAKING A **BUCK** IF HE COULD.

FOR **FIVE** DOLLARS, I'LL PLAY **FOUR** GAMES WITH YOU, GIVING YOU **POINTERS** ALONG THE WAY...

SOUND FAIR?

SURE, ALL RIGHT.

HE ANNOUNCED AND EXPLAINED THE **LOGIC** BEHIND EACH OF HIS MOVES, POINTING OUT THE **INEQUITIES** OF EACH OF MY MOVES ALONG THE WAY— IT WAS A TRULY **HUMBLING** MOMENT.

YOU DO **THAT**, AND I'LL PUT YOU IN **MATE**. MAXIMUM, THREE MOVES.

AW, GEEZ.

BEFORE LONG, I BEGAN TO TELL HIM MY **REASON** FOR VISITING THE PARK THAT DAY.

WHAT DO YOU KNOW ABOUT ANY **CHARACTERS** WHO HAVE PASSED THROUGH HERE?

HE SPOKE **PROUDLY** OF THE CHESS CORNER AND ITS INHABITANTS, LAMENTING THE **DETERIORATION** OF THE SCENE OVER THE YEARS DUE TO **DRUG** PUSHERS.

THIS PLACE HAS **CHANGED** MAN...

I BEGAN TO WORRY THAT I WASN'T GOING TO **UNEARTH** ANYTHING THAT WASN'T ALREADY KNOWN.

ARE THERE ANY INTERESTING **HISTORIES** THAT YOU CAN SHARE WITH ME?

YOU KNOW WHO YOU **NEED** TO TALK TO? YOU NEED TO TALK TO **RICHIE**.

THE MORE TIME I SPENT TALKING TO THE CHESS PLAYERS, THE MORE I REALIZED HOW WELL **RESPECTED** "RICHIE," OR RICHARD PETERSON, WAS.

YEAH, RICHIE'S SEEN **EVERYTHING** — HE'S BEEN PHOTOGRAPHING THIS CORNER SINCE THE **1960's**...

SINCE THE **60's**?! OH YES, THIS IS **DEFINITELY** THE MAN I NEED TO SPEAK TO...

I CAME BACK TO THE CHESS CORNER IN WASHINGTON SQUARE PARK A FEW TIMES, HOPING TO RUN INTO RICHARD, BUT WITH NO **LUCK**.

DO YOU KNOW WHAT **DAYS** OR **TIMES** RICHARD USUALLY COMES AROUND?

WHY DON'T YOU JUST DROP BY HIS **PLACE**? HE LIVES OVER ON THE **BOWERY**.

THE TRUTH IS, I HADN'T GIVEN IT MUCH THOUGHT — I JUST ASSUMED I WOULD HAVE TO RUN INTO HIM IN THE **CHESS** ENVIRONMENT IF I WAS EVER TO MEET HIM.

YEAH MAN, JUST HAVE THE **DUDE** AT THE FRONT DESK CALL UP TO HIS ROOM...

WITH RICHARD'S ADDRESS NOW IN MY POSSESSION, I WENT THE FOLLOWING WEEKEND OVER TO THE BOWERY.

RICHARD LIVED IN THE **WHITE HOUSE HOTEL**, AN OLD HOSTEL WITH SOME PERMANENT CUBICLE UNITS.

WHEN I GOT THERE, IT TURNED OUT THAT THE PERSON AT THE FRONT DESK WAS NOT ABLE TO JUST PHONE UP TO RICHARD.

JUST HANG AROUND THE LOBBY FOR A WHILE — RICHARD'S **ALWAYS** COMING AND GOING...

AFTER AN HOUR OF WAITING AROUND AND SCRIBBLING IN MY SKETCHBOOK, I DECIDED TO ASK THE OLD MEN HANGING AROUND THE LOBBY ABOUT RICHARD.

DO EITHER OF YOU KNOW RICHARD PETERSON?

SURE — RICHARD LIVES **NEXT DOOR** TO ME. HE'S UP THERE — JUST LET ME FINISH MY COFFEE, HERE, AND I'LL GO GET HIM.

AFTER THE GENTLEMAN WHO OFFERED TO HELP ME WENT UPSTAIRS, I SAT AROUND FOR ANOTHER TEN OR FIFTEEN MINUTES.

FINALLY, RICHARD APPEARED FROM THE STAIRWELL DOOR.

HERE WAS **RICHARD PETERSON**, A TALL, HANDSOME MAN, IN GOOD SHAPE FOR A SEVENTY-YEAR-OLD.

MY NEIGHBOR TELLS ME YOU BEEN **LOOKIN'** FOR ME.

I'VE BEEN TOLD **YOU'RE** THE MAN TO TALK TO ABOUT THE **CHESS SCENE** OVER IN WASH SQUARE.

I TOLD RICHARD THAT I WAS IN SEARCH OF SOME **UNIQUE** PERSPECTIVE ABOUT THE CHESS CORNER FOR A STORY I'D LIKE TO WRITE.

I HEAR YOU'VE BEEN PHOTOGRAPHING THOSE GUYS SINCE THE 60'S.

YEAH, BUT MOST OF MY NEGATIVES WERE **STOLEN** A WHILE BACK.

FROM THIS VERY **LOBBY!**

I WAS MOVING ROOMS, AND MY THINGS WERE STACKED UP IN **THIS** HALLWAY FOR A FEW HOURS.

WHEN I CAME BACK, **EVERYTHING** WAS **GONE.**

THAT'S RIGHT — MOST OF THE PHOTOS I'VE GOT LEFT ARE FROM THE **MID-90'S** TO THE PRESENT.

GOOD **LORD!** ALL OF THOSE PHOTOS... **GONE!**

I FELT THE BOTTOM **FALLING** OUT OF A POTENTIALLY GREAT STORY.

>SIGH<

CAN YOU SHARE SOME OF THE PHOTOS YOU **DO HAVE** WITH ME?

I'D ALSO **LOVE** TO HEAR ANY STORIES YOU MIGHT HAVE ABOUT THE CHESS CORNER & THE **PEOPLE** WHO HANG OUT THERE.

RICHARD OBLIGED AND WENT UPSTAIRS TO GET SOME OF HIS PHOTOS.

GEEZ, TOO BAD ABOUT THOSE **PHOTOS** — WELL, HE SEEMS LIKE AN **ARTICULATE** MAN — MAYBE HE'S GOT SOME INTERESTING **STORIES** TO TELL.

RICHARD AND I WENT OVER TO A DINER ON SECOND AVENUE — HE LIKED TO EAT IN THIS DINER EVERY NOW AND THEN — AND WE **PORED** OVER THE PHOTOS.

HERE ARE SOME OF THE **REGULARS** JUST HANGIN' AROUND ON A SUMMER DAY.

THIS GIRL USED TO STOP BY WHEN SHE WAS A **STUDENT** AT **NYU** — WE DIDN'T SEE HER FOR **NINE, TEN** YEARS, THEN SHE CAME BACK ON HER **WEDDING** DAY.

OH, AND **THIS** IS **CUBA** — HE'S THE **BADDEST** HUSTLER OVER THERE.

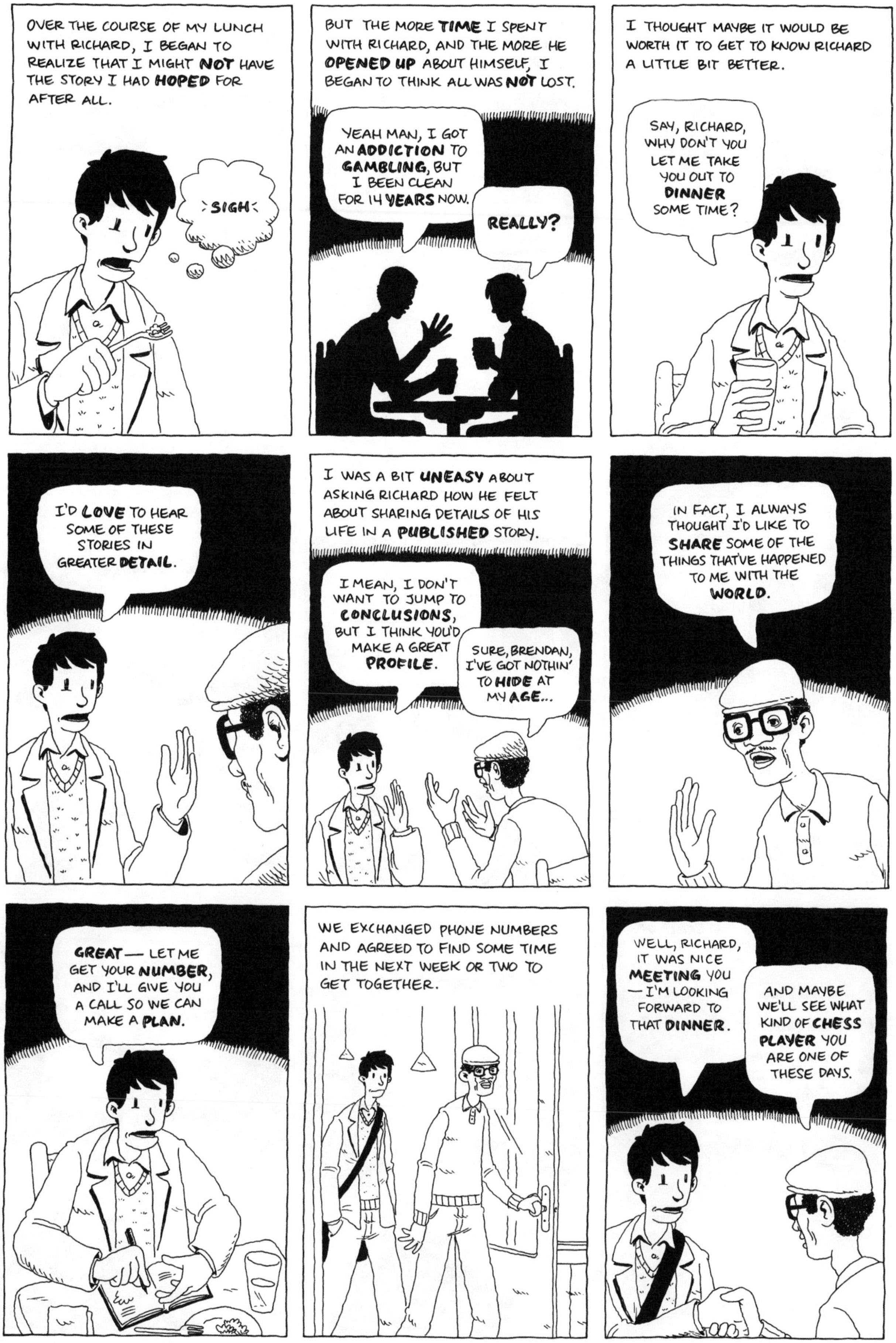

OVER THE COURSE OF MY LUNCH WITH RICHARD, I BEGAN TO REALIZE THAT I MIGHT **NOT** HAVE THE STORY I HAD **HOPED** FOR AFTER ALL.
SIGH
BUT THE MORE **TIME** I SPENT WITH RICHARD, AND THE MORE HE **OPENED UP** ABOUT HIMSELF, I BEGAN TO THINK ALL WAS **NOT** LOST.
YEAH MAN, I GOT AN **ADDICTION** TO **GAMBLING**, BUT I BEEN CLEAN FOR 14 **YEARS** NOW.
REALLY?
I THOUGHT MAYBE IT WOULD BE WORTH IT TO GET TO KNOW RICHARD A LITTLE BIT BETTER.
SAY, RICHARD, WHY DON'T YOU LET ME TAKE YOU OUT TO **DINNER** SOME TIME?
I'D **LOVE** TO HEAR SOME OF THESE STORIES IN GREATER **DETAIL**.
I WAS A BIT **UNEASY** ABOUT ASKING RICHARD HOW HE FELT ABOUT SHARING DETAILS OF HIS LIFE IN A **PUBLISHED** STORY.
I MEAN, I DON'T WANT TO JUMP TO **CONCLUSIONS**, BUT I THINK YOU'D MAKE A GREAT **PROFILE**.
SURE, BRENDAN, I'VE GOT NOTHIN' TO **HIDE** AT MY **AGE**...
IN FACT, I ALWAYS THOUGHT I'D LIKE TO **SHARE** SOME OF THE THINGS THAT'VE HAPPENED TO ME WITH THE **WORLD**.
GREAT— LET ME GET YOUR **NUMBER**, AND I'LL GIVE YOU A CALL SO WE CAN MAKE A **PLAN**.
WE EXCHANGED PHONE NUMBERS AND AGREED TO FIND SOME TIME IN THE NEXT WEEK OR TWO TO GET TOGETHER.
WELL, RICHARD, IT WAS NICE **MEETING** YOU — I'M LOOKING FORWARD TO THAT **DINNER**.
AND MAYBE WE'LL SEE WHAT KIND OF **CHESS PLAYER** YOU ARE ONE OF THESE DAYS.

Panel 1:
I PHONED RICHARD A WEEK LATER TO SEE IF HE WAS AVAILABLE FOR A TUESDAY NIGHT.

HELLO, RICHARD, IT'S ME, BRENDAN— YOU KNOW, THE **CARTOONIST** YOU MET WITH LAST WEEK.

I REMEMBER YOU, BRENDAN— WHAT'S UP, MAN?

Panel 2:
I SUGGESTED WE MEET AT THE **MINETTA TAVERN** — MOSTLY BECAUSE I KNEW WE'D BE ABLE TO SIT DOWN FOR AS LONG AS WE LIKED, WITHOUT THE HOUSE **NUDGING** US OUT.

MINETTA TAVERN RESTAURANT

Panel 3:
RICHARD WAS ALREADY SITTING AT THE BAR WITH HIS **RUM & COKE** WHEN I ARRIVED.

RICHARD...

HEY, BRENDAN!

Panel 4:

CAN I GET YOU SOMETHING TO **DRINK**?

SURE, MACALLAN. **NEAT**, PLEASE.

Panel 5:
WE STAYED FOR A QUICK DRINK AT THE BAR BEFORE WE SAT DOWN FOR DINNER.

SO, WHAT'VE YOU BEEN UP TO?

AW, MAN, THIS DAMN **COMPUTER** HAS BEEN GIVIN' ME **TROUBLE**— I RUN THE MCAFEE OVER AND **OVER**, AND IT'S THE SAME DAMN THING EACH **TIME**...

YOU'VE GOTTA GET A **MAC!**

Panel 6:
THERE'S SOMETHING **COMFORTING** ABOUT THE MINETTA TAVERN — IT'S A REAL **THROWBACK** OF A REST- AURANT, WHICH IS FINE BY ME.

DO YOU HAVE A TABLE FOR **TWO** IN THE BACK ROOM?

RIGHT THIS WAY...

Panel 7:
RICHARD ORDERED THE **SCALLOPS** AND I ORDERED THE **RISOTTO** SPECIAL.

THE **FOOD'S** NOT BAD, BUT IT'S MOSTLY THE **ATMOSPHERE** THAT DOES IT FOR ME.

IT'S A **NICE** ROOM.

Panel 8:
WE GOT TO TALKING ABOUT RICHARD'S **PAST** FAIRLY QUICKLY.

YOU SEE, I'VE ALWAYS BEEN LOOKING FOR THE **EASIEST** PATH — I NEVER WANTED TO **WORK** FOR A LIVING.

Panel 9:

I THINK IT'S A RESULT OF MY DAYS IN **FOSTER** HOMES.

RICHARD WENT ON TO TELL ME HOW THEY **TOOK** HIM AWAY FROM HIS MOTHER WHEN HE WAS **FIVE** BECAUSE THE AUTHORITIES OF THE VERY **AFFLUENT** WESTFIELD, NEW JERSEY, DEEMED HER **UNFIT** TO SUPPORT HIM AND HIS SIBLINGS.

MY MOM DIDN'T HAVE TO WORK AFTER THE PEOPLE WHO EMPLOYED HER **DIED** — THEY LEFT HER THE HOUSE IN THEIR **WILL.**

BUT ALL THE **AUTHORITIES** SAW WAS A WOMAN AT HOME ALL DAY WHO WASN'T **WORKING**, BUT HAD **CHILDREN** TO RAISE.

HE ALSO TOLD ME THAT AFTER HE WAS OUT OF THE MILITARY HE **BOUNCED** FROM JOB TO JOB.

NO JOB COULD KEEP MY **INTEREST** LONGER THAN A COUPLE OF **MONTHS**, SO I WOULD **QUIT** BEFORE LONG...

BUT AFTER A WEEK OR TWO OF NOT WORKING, I WOULD REALIZE THAT I HAD NO **CHOICE** BUT TO GO AND GET ANOTHER JOB.

I KNEW I HAD TO LOOK **GOOD** ON THOSE JOB INTERVIEWS, SO I BOUGHT MYSELF A **CUSTOM** TAILORED HERRINGBONE **SUIT.**

SHARP!

THAT'S RIGHT, BUT IN ADDITION TO INTERVIEWS, THAT GOOD OL' HERRINGBONE **SUIT** BECAME INSTRUMENTAL TO SOME OF THE **HUSTLIN'** I WAS ALSO DOING AT THE TIME.

OH YEAH, WHAT SORT OF STUFF?

HELL, I GOT NOTHIN' TO **HIDE** AT MY AGE...

I HAD A FEW **SCAMS** GOING, LIKE SELLING FUR **COATS** AND **CHEATING** PAY PHONES...

NO KIDDING.

YEAH, THERE WAS **PLENTY** OF WAYS TO MAKE SOME EASY **FOLDING** MONEY.

SO, DO YOU WANT TO **TELL** ME ABOUT SOME OF THESE **STORIES?**

RICHARD SEEMED QUITE **HAPPY** TO SHARE THESE STORIES OF HIS YOUTH, **HUSTLING** ON THE STREETS OF NEW YORK.

WELL, THIS **FRIEND** OF MINE HAD A **MINK** FUR COAT— AN **I.J. FOX** FUR....

IN THOSE DAYS, I.J. FOX WAS **THE** FUR COAT MANUFACTURER.

HE ALSO HAD A **POLICEMAN'S** UNIFORM...

I'D WALK AROUND THE STREETS OF **SOUTH HARLEM** WITH THE COAT, LOOKING FOR A YOUNG **COUPLE** I COULD SELL IT TO...

HEY MY MAN, WHY DON'T YOU CONSIDER BUYING A NICE **COAT** FOR YOUR SWEETHEART? —ONLY **FIFTY** BUCKS.

AFTER A MINUTE OR TWO OF THEM **INSPECTING** THE COAT, THAT I.J. FOX TAG, AND THE GIRL **PLEADING** HER MAN TO **BUY** IT FOR HER, I'D HAVE A SALE.

WOW— **I.J. FOX!**

OOH, REAL **MINK!**

THEN I'D **SPLIT**, AND A FEW MOMENTS LATER, MY FRIEND WOULD **SHOW UP** IN HIS POLICE UNIFORM, WITH HIS GIRLFRIEND PUTTING ON AN ACT.

THAT'S **THEM**, OFFICER! THEY GOT MY **BAG** WITH **MY** COAT!

AND SHE WOULD POINT TO A **TAG** INSIDE WITH HER **NAME** ON IT.

SEE?! I **TOLD** YOU IT WAS **MINE!**

WELL, DO YOU WANT TO PRESS **CHARGES**, MISS?

NO, I JUST WANT MY **COAT** BACK, AND I'LL BE ON MY **WAY!**

THE COUPLE WOULD PROBABLY FIGURE THE COAT WAS **HOT**, AND FELT **LUCKY** THEY WEREN'T GETTING **ARRESTED** FOR POSSESSING IT.

AND WE'D PULL THAT **SCAM** SEVERAL TIMES IN ONE **AFTERNOON**...

WE'D MAKE SIX OR SEVEN **HUNDRED** DOLLARS IN ONE **DAY!**

EVEN WHEN I WAS WORKING A **LEGIT** JOB, I'D FIND WAYS TO **CHEAT** A FEW EXTRA BUCKS.

HOW'S THAT?

I USED TO **SNEAK** PEOPLE INTO BROADWAY SHOWS THROUGH THE BACK DOOR OF A THEATER I USED TO WORK IN—

I'D CHARGE THEM A LITTLE **LESS** THAN TICKET PRICE!

I ALSO USED TO **USHER** AT THE **APOLLO** THEATER UP IN HARLEM, WHERE I'D KEEP THE FIRST ROW OF THE **BALCONY** EMPTY, AND NOT LET PEOPLE SIT THERE.

—I'D TELL THEM IT WAS **RESERVED**.

THEN WHEN IT GOT **CROWDED** UP IN THE BALCONY, I'D **SELL** THOSE SEATS FOR **FIVE BUCKS** EACH!

TELL ME ABOUT THIS PAY PHONE **SCAM** YOU MENTIONED...

OH YEAH, THAT — EVERYONE WAS DOING **THAT**.

THE PAY PHONES WERE **DIFFERENT** BACK THEN...

I THINK THEY **CHANGED** THE PHONES TO THE WAY THEY ARE TODAY BECAUSE OF HOW **EASY** IT WAS TO **CHEAT** THEM BACK THEN.

I'D GO AROUND ABOUT **TWO** OR **THREE** IN THE MORNING AND STICK A BUNCH OF THE PLASTIC WRAPPING FROM **CIGARETTE** PACKAGES UP INSIDE THE COIN RETURNS OF **SEVERAL** PHONES...

THIS WOULD **BLOCK** THE COINS FROM REACHING THE COIN BOX ANYTIME SOMEONE WOULD MAKE A CALL.

THEN I'D GO BACK REAL **EARLY** IN THE MORNING THE NEXT DAY AND TRY TO FIND ANY STRAY STREET-CLEANER **BRISTLES** THAT MIGHT BE LAYING AROUND...

I'D **POKE** THAT BRISTLE UP INSIDE THE PHONE AND **PUNCTURE** THE WRAPPER, AND OUT POURS A LOAD OF **NICKELS** AND **DIMES**—

SOMETIMES SEVEN OR EIGHT **DOLLARS'** WORTH!

THAT REMINDS ME OF **ANOTHER** STORY...

ONE TIME I WAS CHEATING SOME PAY PHONES IN THE BASEMENT OF A BIG **MIDTOWN HOTEL** — I HAD ON MY HERRINGBONE SUIT, AND I WAS FEELING **GOOD** ABOUT MYSELF WITH THAT THING ON, SO I WENT UPSTAIRS TO THE **LOBBY**...

AS I PASSED THE FRONT DESK, I COULD SEE THE **ROOM KEYS** HANGING IN THEIR BOX...

EXCUSE ME, COULD I HAVE MY ROOM KEY, PLEASE? —ROOM 2220.

THE MAN BEHIND THE DESK DIDN'T HESITATE, AND GAVE ME THE **KEY** — THEN I **FAKED** A GESTURE AS IF I FORGOT SOMETHING OUTSIDE, AND I WENT AROUND TO THE **BASEMENT** ENTRANCE.

I PHONED THE HOTEL OPERATOR FROM ONE OF THE **PHONE BOOTHS**.

YES, CAN I HAVE MR. FIELDS IN ROOM 2220, PLEASE?

WE DON'T HAVE A MR. FIELDS IN ROOM 2220, BUT A MR. CHANDLER — THERE DOESN'T SEEM TO BE AN ANSWER...

KNOWING THE ROOM WAS **EMPTY**, I TOOK THE ELEVATOR UP FROM THE BASEMENT TO ROOM 2220 AND **LIFTED** WHAT I COULD.

I MADE OFF WITH A **CAMERA**, SOME **BINOCULARS** AND SOME **CLOTHES** THAT DAY.

LATER THAT DAY I **SOLD** THAT ROOM KEY TO A **HUSTLER** IN MIDTOWN.

HEY, FIFTY BUCKS FOR THIS **ROOM KEY** — ALL YOU GOTTA DO IS PHONE UP AND MAKE SURE NOBODY'S IN THE ROOM...

ALL RIGHT, YEAH!

IT WAS A **STRANGE** DAY — IT WAS AS IF I WAS BEING **GUIDED** BY AN **INVISIBLE HAND** THAT AFTERNOON — I DIDN'T KNOW WHAT I WAS **DOING**.

RICHARD AND I FINISHED UP OUR DINNER AT THE MINETTA TAVERN THAT NIGHT AND HEADED ACROSS TOWN ON BLEECKER STREET.

SO TELL ME A LITTLE BIT ABOUT THOSE GUYS OVER AT THE CHESS CORNER...

MOST OF 'EM ARE **HUSTLIN'** SO THEY CAN HAVE SOME MONEY TO FEED THEIR **ADDICTION** — WHATEVER THAT MAY BE...

MY ADDICTION IS **GAMBLING** — BUT I'VE BEEN CLEAN FOR **FOURTEEN** YEARS.

I WAS ADDICTED TO GAMBLING AT **POKER**, BUT I DIDN'T KNOW WHAT I WAS **DOING**...

I DIDN'T KNOW THE PERCENTAGES AND I WAS **TELEGRAPHING** MY HANDS — BUT I WAS **BLINDED** BY THE THRILL OF WINNING THE OCCASIONAL BIG HAND!

ONCE I **REALIZED** THIS, I KNEW I DIDN'T WANT TO BE SEEN AS A **CHUMP**, SO I CUT IT **OUT**.

SO WHY DO YOU KEEP COMING BACK TO THE PARK TO PLAY CHESS?

MOSTLY FOR FOLDING MONEY — PAYS FOR CIGARETTES.

I CAN MAKE FIFTY OR **SIXTY BUCKS** ON A SATURDAY OVER THERE!

I **DID** FIND AN INTERESTING STORY AFTER ALL — **AND** I FOUND A NEW **FRIEND**.

I STILL SEE RICHARD EVERY NOW AND THEN — MOSTLY AT THE **CHESS SHOP** DOWN ON THOMPSON STREET, WHERE HE CONTINUES TO MAKE ME LOOK LIKE A **FOOL** AT THE CHESS BOARD.

YOU'RE IN CHECK IN **TWO** MOVES — DO YOU SEE IT?

SYNCOPATED
AN ANTHOLOGY OF NONFICTION PICTO-ESSAYS

THE CONTRIBUTORS

NICK BERTOZZI

Nick Bertozzi has written and drawn many comics over the years. You can read many of his stories at www.nickbertozzi.com. He lives in New York City with his wife and daughters.

BRENDAN BURFORD

Brendan Burford, editor of this book, previously edited and self-published three volumes of *Syncopated*. By day, Brendan is the comics editor of King Features Syndicate. He enjoys old comics, old records, and old sailboats.

JIM CAMPBELL

Jim Campbell grew up in the heart of the heartland in Iowa. He now lives in Brooklyn, New York, where he makes comics, takes 3D photographs, and plays noisy rock music in a band called *Paper Fleet*. His drawings can be found in various anthologies like this one as well as in his own series, *Krachmacher*.

GREG COOK

Greg Cook is a Boston artist, newspaperman, and garbageman. His darkly funny comic book *Catch as Catch Can* was published by Highwater Books in 2001. He is slowly working on a documentary graphic novel for First Second Books about Massachusetts veterans of the war in Iraq. Visit gregcookland.com.

SARAH GLIDDEN

Sarah Glidden is the creator of *How to Understand Israel in 60 Days or Less,* the self-published first chapters of which earned her the Masie Kukoc Award and an Ignatz Award for Promising New Talent. She is currently living in Brooklyn, New York, where she is working on the full-length version of this book, forthcoming from Vertigo. Visit her website at www.smallnoises.com.

RICHARD AND BRIAN HAIMES

Richard and Brian Haimes are father and son. Richard is an oral surgeon with a great passion for fly-fishing. Brian is an animator, puppet maker, and occasional cartoonist. You can see more of Brian's work on his website, www.brianhaimes.com.

ALEX HOLDEN

Alex Holden grew up in Baltimore. His ongoing comic is called *Magic Hour.* You can see his illustrations and comics at www.alexholden.com. His other interests include Fender guitars, early 70s New York graffiti writing, and walking around in the Ridgewood Reservoir. He lives in Brooklyn with his wife, Mary.

PAUL HOPPE

Paul Hoppe was born in Poland and grew up in the sunny south of Germany, where he studied graphic design and fine arts. Eventually, Paul moved to New York City to pursue his MFA in illustration at the School of Visual Arts. He liked the city so much that he stayed. Paul's illustrations have appeared in many newspapers and magazines, including *The New York Times* and *The New Yorker*. He has worked on animated series for German television and national ad campaigns for Adidas and IBM. He has published two graphic novels in Germany and has co-founded the comic anthology *Rabid Rabbit*. Paul illustrated the children's book *Metal Man* by Aaron Reynolds and wrote and illustrated the picture book *Hat*.

PAUL KARASIK

Paul Karasik is the co-creator of the graphic novels *City of Glass* and *The Ride Together: A Brother and Sister's Memoir of Autism in the Family*. His latest book, *I Shall Destroy All the Civilized Planets: The Comics of Fletcher Hanks* (www.fletcherhanks.com), won an Eisner Award. *The New Yorker* and *Nickelodeon* magazines have run his gag cartoons.

VICTOR MARCHAND KERLOW

Victor M. Kerlow was born, raised, and educated in New York City and continues to live there, drawing full time. He has worked on a range of projects for magazines, comics, book publishers, ad agencies, and film studios. His clients include *The New Yorker* and *The New York Times,* and his work has been included in the Society of Illustrators. More of his work can be viewed online at www.victorkerlow.com.

DAVE KIERSH

Dave Kiersh is an illustrator and cartoonist. He has also worked as a teacher and librarian. His books include *A Last Cry For Help* (2006), *Neverland* (2008), and *Dirtbags, Mall Chicks and Motorbikes* (2009). Originally from Long Island, he currently lives in Massachusetts. More of his work can be found online at www.davekcomics.com.

ALEC LONGSTRETH

Alec Longstreth has been self-publishing his minicomic, *Phase 7,* since 2002 and intends to continue doing so until his death. In 2005, *Phase 7* won the Ignatz Award for Outstanding Minicomic. That same year, Alec co-authored *The Dvorak Zine,* an informational comic about the Dvorak Simplified Keyboard, which has been featured on BoingBoing.net and Slashdot.org. Alec is currently a fellow at the Center for Cartoon Studies in Vermont, where he is working on his first graphic novel, *Basewood*. Visit www.DVzine.org and www.alec-longstreth.com

JOSH NEUFELD

Josh Neufeld is a cartoonist, illustrator, and the author of *A.D.: New Orleans After the Deluge* (Pantheon, 2009), a true story of Hurricane Katrina. Shortly after the hurricane, Neufeld spent three weeks as an American Red Cross volunteer in Biloxi, Mississippi. The blog entries he kept about that experience turned into a self-published book and indirectly led to *A.D.,* a good part of which was originally serialized in *SMITH Magazine*. Neufeld also wrote and drew the Xeric Award–winning graphic travelogue *A Few Perfect Hours*. Born in New York City, Neufeld lives in Brooklyn with his wife and daughter.

RINA PICCOLO

Rina was born in Toronto, Canada. Her syndicated comic strip, *Tina's Groove,* appears in over one hundred daily newspapers. She is also a contributor to the syndicated comic strip *Six Chix*. Rina's gag cartoons have appeared in *The New Yorker* and *Parade* magazine. Rina enjoys collecting old postcards, listening in on conversations taking place in public, and talking to her pet canary, Olive.

NATE POWELL

Nate Powell was born in 1978 in Little Rock, Arkansas. He started publishing comics in 1992 and graduated from the School of Visual Arts in 2000. His books include *Swallow Me Whole* (Top Shelf, 2008), *Please Release* (Top Shelf, 2006), *Sounds of Your Name* (Microcosm, 2006), *It Disappears* (Soft Skull, 2004), *Tiny Giants* (Soft Skull, 2003), and the *Walkie Talkie* series (self-published, 2000-02). Nate has also worked full-time for adults with developmental disabilities since 1999. He ran Harlan records out of his bedroom for many years, and played in punk rock bands *Soophie Nun Squad, Wait, Divorce Chord, Boomfancy,* and *Gioteens*. Nate loves breakfast.

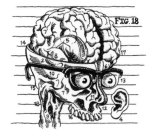

TRICIA VAN DEN BERGH

Born 1978. Is currently aboard the maritime vessel RV *Ursa Minor* participating in an inquiry concerning a possible fourth splinter to the Hermetic Order of the Golden Dawn, the Golden Orb. Likes cats.